J 641.5 ISA
Isaac, Andrew.
Cooks and kids. 3 : top chefs
and kids cook up a storm with
Gregg Wallace

MAR -- 2017

D1297819

Cooks & Kids 3
Published in Great Britain in
2016 by Graffeg Limited.

Written by Andrew Isaac
and Gregg Wallace
Copyright © 2016.
Photography by National
Fostering Agency Limited
Copyright © 2016.
Designed and produced by
Graffeg Limited Copyright
© 2016

Graffeg Limited, 24 Stradey
Park Business Centre, Mwrwg
Road, Llangennech, Llanelli,
Carmarthenshire SA14 8YP
Wales UK Tel 01554 824000
www.graffeg.com

Graffeg are hereby identified
as the authors of this work in
accordance with section 77 of
the Copyrights, Designs and
Patents Act 1988.

A CIP Catalogue record for
this book is available from the
British Library.

All rights reserved. No
part of this publication
may be reproduced, stored
in a retrieval system or
transmitted, in any form or
by any means, electronic,
mechanical, photocopying,
recording or otherwise, without
the prior permission
of the publishers.

National Fostering Agency Ltd
Frays Court
71 Cowley Road
Uxbridge
Middlesex, UB8 2AE
Tel: 01895 200 300
www.nfa.co.uk
Cooks&Kids@nfa.co.uk

Graffeg and the National
Fostering Agency Group would
like to thank the following
companies for their
invaluable support:

AVEQIA
For supplying an excellent
venue, catering supplies and
fantastic services and support
throughout the entire project.

Brakes
For arranging and supplying
most of the food and
ingredients.

CCS
For supplying us with the
brilliant chef's whites and
aprons.

Miranda Parry Photography
For taking the most amazing
photographs.

Duncan Smith
For kind support with the video
productions.

STEEL London
For developing and building our
Cooks & Kids website:
www.cooksandkids.com

Pure Emerald
For arranging social media
activities.

Halstan UK
For kindly printing and
providing the Cooks & Kids
application form.

Fairfax Meadow
For arranging and supplying
the majority of the meat and
poultry.

CocoPacific Virgin Coconut Oil
For the coconut oil of which
Aldo Zilli is an ambassador for.

Pasta Garofalo
For the pasta ingredients and
for the gifts given to children
from Sara Danesin Medio.

John Woodward
For his expert chef consultancy.

Cook & Kids is a registered
trademark.

ISBN 9781910862735

1 2 3 4 5 6 7 8 9

Top chefs and kids cook up a storm with Gregg Wallace

Cooks & Kids 3™

Bookmobile
Fountaindale Public Library
Bolingbrook, IL
(630) 759-2102

GRAFFEG

CONTENTS

The trademarks and brands mentioned in this book are the property of their respective owners, and no claim is made to them and no endorsement of this book is implied or claimed.

FOREWORD

It gives me great pleasure to welcome you to *Cooks & Kids 3*.

Our Cooks & Kids projects have become extremely popular and we have been delighted with the participation from the children and young people who are all part of the NFA Group family.

As the largest independent foster care provider in the United Kingdom, we are, at NFA Group, totally committed, not only through our front line professional social work staff, but through all our field and office-based support teams, to improve the quality of life for the children and young people in our care each and every single day.

Our project continues with its aim to encourage young people to get interested in food and, importantly, learn how to cook. *Cooks & Kids 3* is full of great recipes, created not only by the NFA Group foster and birth children, aged from six to eighteen, but with some fantastic contributions from the celebrities and celebrity chefs that have given their time and their talent to support our project.

I would like to thank a team of people – namely my CSR team, our participating chefs, our guest celebrities and social workers and support teams, and of course, the children and young people – for making *Cooks & Kids 3* such a great project.

In particular, my sincere thanks must go to Gregg Wallace who has helped tirelessly with his support and his time to make sure this edition is the best yet.

On page 154 you will find a full list of all those individuals and organisations that have supported and contributed to making this happen. My personal thanks must also go to Paul Vine and the team at Avegia, who kindly opened their doors and their hearts to us by giving us the run of their amazing event venue and cookery studio in London's St Bride's Street.

We are delighted that the royalties from the sales of this book will continue to be donated to Place2Be with the aim of assisting founder Benita Refson and her team in their work. Their work helps children cope with a wide range of complex social issues including bereavement, family breakdown, bullying, domestic violence, neglect and trauma, so that they can thrive and achieve their potential, both in and outside the classroom.

I hope you enjoy *Cooks & Kids 3* and enjoy making the recipes the youngsters and chefs have created for you to try, in the knowledge that you have also helped make a difference to a youngster somewhere in the UK.

Enjoy the book.

Iain Anderson, Group Chief Executive, National Fostering Agency Group

National Fostering Agency Group

Founded in 1995, the NFA Group provides high quality foster care that places children and young people at the heart of everything they do.

NFA Group works with local authorities and foster carers throughout the UK to create the best possible opportunities and outcomes for children. It is the foster carer provider of choice for many local authorities across the UK. The group employs experienced and professionally qualified staff and only recruits the very best foster carers, providing them with effective, on-going training to continually develop their skills and knowledge.

Programmes are implemented to monitor and manage each foster care placement, working to each child's individually tailored care plan. Foster carers have access to social workers 24 hours a day, 7 days a week. NFA Group is totally committed to the improvement of outcomes for every child it looks after and can demonstrate the real impact of the care it provides. Outcomes and individual placement recordings for each child are securely recorded and the information is freely available to all placing authorities.

NFA Group is proud to collaborate with so many local and dedicated foster carers, without whom the service would not exist. Partnering with its long-serving carers and its dedicated professional team, NFA Group is proud to add to the quality of daily life for those children and young people in its care.

If you want to learn more about being a foster carer call 0800 044 3030 or visit www.nfa.co.uk.

. . . .

'I feel hugely privileged to be working with the kids on the project. It was great to see how cooking brings out the confidence in these kids and I'm so proud to be part of that!'
Ping Coombes, Winner of *MasterChef* 2014

'My wife and I had a great time with NFA and the Cooks & Kids team, the whole of Aveqia was buzzing with laughter and, wow, some really good cooking going on!'
Tom Kerridge

'I have enjoyed working with the NFA Group on their Cooks & Kids project. What a vehicle to allow children and young people to channel their energy, learn about food and contribute to something that will help children more disadvantaged than themselves!'
Gregg Wallace

PLACE2BE

Place2Be is a UK registered charity, dedicated to enhancing the wellbeing and prospects of children and their families by providing access to therapeutic and emotional support in schools.

Sometimes life can be tough for children and they need someone to talk to. Place2Be provides school-based emotional and mental health support services to ensure children have just that. Working in 205 schools across the UK, supporting 75,000 children, their parents, carers and school staff, Place2Be supports children to cope with a wide range of complex social issues including bereavement, family breakdown, bullying, domestic violence, neglect and trauma, so that they can thrive and achieve their potential both in and outside of the classroom. The charity also provides support to parents and carers, knowing this to be truly beneficial in helping children and families to overcome problems.

There is a real and growing need to support children's emotional and mental health. One in ten children aged between 5 and 16 years has a mental health problem, and many carry these problems with them into adulthood. Half of those with lifetime mental health problems first experience symptoms by the age of 14. Among teenagers, the rate of depression and anxiety has increased by 70% in the past 25 years. Ten years ago, detailed estimates put the costs of mental health problems in England at £77 billion, including costs of lost productivity and the wider impacts on well being. More recent estimates suggest the cost may be closer to £105 billion. Place2Be believes the case for giving children support early on is clear – and the benefits are reaped not just by the child in question but also by society as a whole.

Since April 2013, Place2Be has been delighted to have the support of HRH The Duchess of Cambridge as the charity's Royal Patron. The Duchess has clearly expressed her commitment to the cause: 'I strongly believe that the issue of mental health problems for young people has to be tackled. Too many young people are suffering from emotional problems, and the impact can be simply devastating.'

Place2Be and National Fostering Agency Group are keen to continue to develop the awareness of the Cooks & Kids project.

'Children are at the heart of everything the two organisations do, we both support children who are facing tough, challenging times. Funds raised through the Cooks & Kids project will help us to reach even more vulnerable children and families so they view their lives with a sense of hope.'

Dame Benita Refson DBE
Place2Be's President and Founding Trustee.

GALLERY

INTRODUCTION

As ever, the Cooks & Kids concept has grown from strength to strength and the premise of 'Time and Talent' has served us well with all those involved giving up their time or using their talent at no cost whatsoever, which, coupled with the generosity of some fantastic suppliers, enabled *Cooks & Kids 3* to fly.

· ·

So how does Cooks & Kids happen – what's it all about? The Cooks & Kids team at NFA Group invited foster children from all over the UK to submit their favourite recipes for the final cook off. Finalists were invited to team up with celebrity chefs Tom Kerridge, Michel Roux Jr, Aldo Zilli, Cyrus Todiwala, Sophie Thompson and many others to cook the recipes together. Gregg Wallace, *MasterChef* judge, tasted the dishes and gave his comments to the cooks and kids. The whole process was written, photographed and published into this book *Cooks & Kids 3* for children everywhere to share the joy of cooking.

· ·

As ever, a passion for food, fun and education is a cornerstone for Cooks & Kids; to engage with children and young people and open their imagination to the boundless possibilities of food. We wanted to channel their creativity into crafting their favourite dishes or inventing recipes around the ingredients they like.

National Fostering Agency Group (NFA Group) is as proud as it can possibly be of the outcomes of the children and young people in its care and is always seeking ways to enable looked after children and the birth children of its carers to contribute to the key tenets of 'Every Child Matters':

· be healthy
· stay safe
· enjoy and achieve
· make a positive contribution
· achieve economic well-being.

Cooks & Kids 'ticks the box' on a number of these, particularly making a positive contribution. Looked after children in foster care do not want to be labelled, they want a normal life, to take part in everyday normal things and, most of all, want to be in a caring environment. Most looked after children are where they are, generally through no fault of their own, and the support they receive within a foster care setting is about them and what they need to rebuild their self-esteem and often their trust in others. Preparing food for others is a great way to show how much you care and that simple fact is probably what makes Cooks & Kids work as an idea and go a long way to helping mend some of that lack of self-esteem and trust.

NFA Group foster carers are amazing in terms of their commitment to the children and young people in our joint care and clearly focus on each child's individual needs. Foster

Gregg Wallace and Michel Roux Jr.

children do not go without the everyday comforts of living; they are warm, clean and safe, have good clothes and, very importantly, are encouraged to eat well. This is all part of the process of preparing them to either go back to their families or, if they are in long-term placement, prepare them for moving into successful adult independence and achieve economic well being.

As a result, the birth and foster children in the NFA Group family are always keen to 'give back' and, in joining in with our project, are actively making a choice and a difference in helping us raise funds for Place2Be. As a charity they provide emotional and therapeutic services in primary and secondary schools, building children's resilience through talking, creative work and play.

In 1989, as a country, the UK fully signed up to the United Nations Convention on the Rights of the Child which is the most complete statement of children's rights ever produced and is the most widely-ratified international human rights treaty in history.

The Convention has 54 articles that cover all aspects of a child's life and set out the civil, political, economic, social and cultural rights that all children everywhere are entitled to. It also explains how adults and governments must work together to make sure all children can enjoy all their rights.

Article twelve states:
"Parties shall assure to the child who is capable of forming his or her own views the right to express those views freely in all matters affecting the child, the views of the child being given due weight in accordance with the age and maturity of the child."

In addition, article thirteen tells us:
"The child shall have the right to freedom of expression; this right shall include freedom

Gregg Wallace, Nia and Michel Roux Jr.

Cyrus Todiwala and Emma.

to seek, receive and impart information and ideas of all kinds, regardless of frontiers, either orally, in writing or in print, in the form of art, or through any other media of the child's choice."

The importance of these two articles is fundamental in guiding those responsible for delivering services to children and young people on how they should approach their work and recognise the voice of the child.

Cooks & Kids 3 is bigger and better than ever before, thanks in no small part to Gregg Wallace's sheer determination to make a real difference to this project and encourage those with whom he works to join in the fun. Well known Michelin starred chefs, winners from *MasterChef* and *Celebrity MasterChef* all joined in the spirit of bringing fun and joy to cooking with kids. They joined some Cooks & Kids stalwarts such as our Consulting Head

Chef John Woodward and Chris Lee from the Bildeston Crown... when you are as busy as some of our guest chefs, giving up one of your precious days off needs a lot of thinking about... and we are so thankful.

Put quite simply, it has enabled the professional world of celebrity chefs and NFA Group's fostered and birth children to get engaged with each other, have huge amounts of fun and work together to create a child-centric book to help disadvantaged children worse off than themselves.

The support and feedback from everyone involved during the course of this project has been remarkable. Without exception, everyone has been enthusiastic and offered assistance in a variety of ways. We are grateful to them all.

As we are sure you will see from some of the pictures in the book, the youngsters were

Left to right: Tom Dell, Sophie Thompson, Kelly Snowdon, Ping Coombes, Gregg Wallace and Chris Lee.

thrilled at the *MasterChef* style feedback they were given 'Gregg Wallace' style. Head to Cooksandkids.com to see some behind the scenes videos and photoshoots.

Thank you for buying this book and we do hope you will enter the spirit of how Cooks & Kids came about. Cooking is fun. Fun food does not have to be junk food. Just try these recipes. And, of course, if you have a recipe you feel we should throw into the pot for the future, and then just let us know. For us "too many cooks" does not apply. The more the merrier!

Bon Appétit.

Andrew Isaac and Gregg Wallace

Mackenzy, Franky & Jay Ruehle.

19

RECIPES

FISH

TROUT PÂTÉ WITH FLATBREADS

 Prep time: 15 minutes   **Cook time:** 45 minutes   **Serves:** 4 people

250g of plain flour

1 tsp of fine salt

1 tbsp olive oil

150ml of warm water

3 spring onions, finely sliced

450g of hot-smoked trout

250g quark (or any soft cheese)

1 pinch of pink peppercorns (plus extra to serve)

a dash of Tabasco

To make the pâté:

1. Put the trout into a pan with most of the chopped spring onions and cook for a minute, or until it is completely opaque. After this, transfer the trout into a bowl with the soft cheese, Tabasco sauce and pink peppercorns. Finally, put the pâté into small serving pots and place the pink peppercorns and the rest of the spring onions on top.

2. Once you have finished, place it in the fridge.

To make the flatbread:

1. Put the flour, oil, salt and warm water into a bowl and mix together. When it is mixed, put it onto the counter and knead for 5 minutes, or until it is elastic.

2. Put the ball of dough to one side and allow it to rest under a bowl for about 15 minutes. Once it has finished resting, roll it into a sausage shape and cut into 8 equal pieces.

3. Roll each of the 8 pieces into a small, thin circle. Heat a flat pan on a medium heat and then cook each circle of dough until it is puffed up or golden brown. Finally, if you want to, cut up the flatbread and serve it with the pâté as a starter or a snack.

FISH PIE

 Prep time: 40 minutes **Cook time:** 30 minutes **Serves:** 2 to 4 people

300g fresh prawns

200g diced salmon

200g coley/pollock, diced

100g smoked haddock, diced

500g of shallots

1 litre of fish stock

1 litre of cream

knob of butter

½ glass of white wine

100g frozen peas

chopped parsley

squeeze of lemon

400g white potatoes

dollop of cream and butter

Parmesan to taste

1. Sweat off the shallots in a little butter then add the wine and reduce.

2. Add the fish stock and reduce.

3. Add the cream and simmer until thickened.

4. Add all of the fish and prawns and continue to stir.

5. Meanwhile, peel and chop the potatoes then add to a saucepan of boiling water.

6. Boil for around 20 minutes, or until soft.

7. Mash the potatoes and mix with a dollop of cream and butter until soft and creamy.

8. When the fish mixture is cooked, add the peas, parsley and lemon to taste.

9. Pour the fish mixture into an oval dish and cover with the mashed potato.

10. Sprinkle Parmesan on top and serve hot, hot, hot!

Leala & Aldo Zilli

TERIYAKI SALMON

 Prep time: 10 minutes   **Cook time:** 20 minutes   **Serves:** 2-4 people

To make Teriyaki sauce

1. While the rice and fish cook, place the soy sauce, rice vinegar, brown sugar, honey, ginger and garlic into a small saucepan and place over a low heat.

2. Bring to the boil, stirring constantly. Allow to boil for 1 minute, the sauce should start to thicken.

3. Place 1 salmon fillet on each plate. Share out the rice with equal amounts onto each plate, gently coat the salmon with the sauce and add your choice of vegetables.

185g rice

4 salmon fillets

½ cup low-salt soy sauce

2 tbsp rice vinegar

3 tsp brown sugar

1 tbsp honey

3/4 tsp ground ginger

1 garlic clove, mashed

selection of vegetables e.g. green beans, carrots, broccoli

To cook the rice and salmon

1. Preheat the oven to 160°C/ Gas 3. Boil water in a saucepan and add the rice.

2. Place the fillets of salmon onto an oven tray, put into the oven.

3. Leave the rice and fillets to cook for 15 minutes, or until ready.

Elliot & Chris Lee
SCAMPI

 Prep time: 25 minutes   **Cook time:** 20 minutes   **Serves:** 4 people

1 bag of large prawns

panko bread crumbs

3 eggs

200g flour

200g baby onions, blanched, peeled and halved

1 English lettuce, shredded

500g fresh peas, podded

200ml chicken stock, reduced to a glaze – 4 tablespoons

8 mint leaves

butter

squeeze of lemon

200ml double cream

vegetable oil for deep frying

chips to serve

1. Preheat the oven to 180°C/ Gas 4. Sauté the onions in a large pan in butter until golden.

2. Add the stock to the sauté pan and reduce to the glaze. Then add the lettuce and cook until soft.

3. Turn the heat down to low-to-medium and add the cream and simmer.

4. Put the eggs into a bowl and beat with a fork. Put the flour into another bowl, and the bread crumbs into another.

5. Toss the prawns first in the flour, then the beaten egg, then the panko bread crumbs.

6. Fry the scampi until golden then put in the oven for 8 minutes.

7. When the sauce has thickened, add the peas, mint and a squeeze of lemon and simmer for a few minutes to warm through.

8. Serve the scampi and sauce on top of chips.

Kai & Chris Lee

STONE BASS
WITH ARTICHOKE PUREE AND ASPARAGUS

 Prep time: 1 hour   **Cook time:** 30 minutes **Serves:** 4 people

4 x 8 oz fillets of bass – stone or sea bass

8 Jersey Royal potatoes – peeled and blanched

handful of tomatoes

bunch of asparagus

bunch of baby artichokes (alternatively use marinated baby artichokes)

handful of carrots, peeled and diced

a celeriac, chopped

splash of white wine

four cloves of garlic, crushed

splash of olive oil

Artichoke purée:

Jerusalem artichokes

chicken stock (enough to cover in pan)

500ml full fat milk

1. Blanch the asparagus in salted water.

2. For the baby artichokes: peel and simmer in olive oil, white wine, carrots and celeriac – all diced – or use the marinated version.

3. For the artichoke purée: Sauté the Jerusalem artichokes in butter – cover with chicken stock and cook until tender.

4. Add 500ml of full fat milk and blend until smooth – you can then pass through a fine sieve. Season to taste.

Confit tomatoes

1. Blanch the tomatoes and remove the skin and seeds.

2. Slice into petal shapes.

Fish

1. Pat the fish fillets dry with kitchen paper – season with salt and pepper.

2. Pan fry the fillets in olive oil, skin side down until crispy.

3. Turn over and cook for 2 minutes, then baste with a knob of butter.

4. Assemble dish as per picture.

PAN FRIED SEA BASS
AND SEXY FRIED EGGS

Prep time: 20 minutes   **Cook time:** 20 minutes   **Serves:** 2 people

Sea Bass

2 sea bass fillets, skin on

3 tbsp oil

1 tbsp cornflour

pinch of sea salt

1 tbsp kecap manis

some coriander leaves to garnish

Sexy fried eggs

4 very good quality eggs

2 spring onions, chopped

1 red chilli, chopped

10g ginger, finely diced

1 1/2 tbsp kecap manis

1 tbsp oil

Sea Bass

1. Place the cornflour on a tray and sprinkle on some salt. Coat the fillets with a light covering of cornflour.

2. Heat the oil in a frying pan, shake off any excess of cornflour, place the fish in the pan, skin side down, and fry for 2 minutes. Do not move the fish.

3. Flip to the opposite side and continue to fry for another 1 1/2 minutes. Cook for a little longer if the fillets are thick. Turn off the heat and let the fillets sit in the pan for another 30 seconds.

4. Place on a plate, drizzle kecap manis onto the fillets and pour 3/4 of the oil from the pan onto the fillets. It will sizzle.

5. Garnish with torn coriander.

Sexy fried eggs

1. Heat oil in a non-stick pan and fry the eggs sunny side up till the edges are crispy. Remove onto a plate.

2. Using the same pan, fry the spring onions, chillies and ginger until they are softened. Sprinkle the mixture on top of the eggs Drizzle over the kecap manis.

MEAT

Zahra & Tom Kerridge

TRAY BAKE CHICKEN

 Prep time: 25 minutes   **Cook time:** 25 minutes   **Serves:** 4 people

4 x chicken breasts

2 red onions cut into ¼

600g mixed seasonal tomatoes, cut into different shape and sizes

1 tsp sea salt

100ml extra virgin olive oil

30g pitted black olives

300g buffalo mozzarella

½ tsp dried oregano

8 slices of Milano salami

1 garlic clove, sliced

1 tbsp raw polenta

1. Preheat the oven to 200°C/ Gas 6. Cut the chicken breasts in half and lightly season. Next, arrange them into a 25cm oven dish.

2. In a bowl add the dried oregano, olives, sliced garlic and tomato, drizzle with a little olive and toss together.

3. Add the dressed tomatoes to the chicken, pushing around the chicken, exposing the skin so it crisps up.

4. Top the tray bake off with the onion quarters, mozzarella and salami, sprinkle over the polenta and place into the oven for 20-25 minutes. After this time the chicken will be cooked, the onions will be charred and the cheese beautifully melted.

5. Remove from the oven and give another drizzle of olive oil and serve.

Lucy & John Woodward

PANKO BREAD CRUMB CHICKEN STRIPS
WITH CREAMY PANCETTA AND MUSHROOM SPAGHETTI

 Prep time: 30 minutes   **Cook time:** 20 minutes   **Serves:** 4 people

4 chicken breasts, skinless

100g flour

2 eggs, beaten

200g panko bread crumbs

500g spaghetti

1 onion, diced

250g mushrooms of your choice

100g pancetta, cut into small 1cm lardons

200ml double cream

a few leaves of chopped parsley

salt and pepper

oil for deep frying

1. Start by slicing the chicken into strips.

2. Toss first in the flour, then beaten eggs, then panko bread crumbs.

3. To make the pasta, cook the spaghetti in boiling water until soft but not overcooked.

4. While the spaghetti is cooking, fry the onion in a little oil until soft.

5. Add the pancetta and mushrooms to the onion and cook until brown.

6. Add the double cream and reduce by half.

7. Fry the chicken in a deep fat fryer or pan fry until golden brown and cooked.

8. Finish the pasta by covering with the mushroom sauce, seasoning with salt and pepper and adding the chopped parsley.

9. Serve the golden chicken strips on the creamy pasta with a few more leaves of parsley.

Austin & John Woodward

Spicy Beef and Mozzarella Pizza

 Prep time: 45 minutes   **Cook time:** 20 minutes   **Serves:** 8-10 slices

For the pizza dough

400g OO flour

100g polenta

1 tsp salt

10g dried yeast

2 tbsp olive oil

320ml warm water

For the tomato sauce

½ onion, chopped

2 garlic cloves, chopped

300g chopped tinned tomatoes

100g tomato puree

6 leaves basil

seasoning

For the topping

200g beef striploin, cut into strips

25g chilli flakes

100g buffalo mozzarella

50g grated Parmesan

10 basil leaves

1. Dissolve the yeast in the warm water.

2. Add all the dough ingredients together and mix until it forms a soft dough.

3. Rest the dough for 20 minutes, allowing it to prove and expand. While it rests, marinate your beef strips in the chilli flakes with a little olive oil.

4. For the sauce, add the onions and garlic to a pan and cook at a low temperature, taking care that they don't brown.

5. Add the tomatoes and tomato puree and reduce until a thick sauce, season and add basil leaves.

6. Preheat the oven to 200°C/ Gas 6. Add your marinated beef strips to a hot pan with a little oil. Brown the beef a little but do not cook through.

7. Take the pizza dough and knead (mix) again until soft, roll out into a large 12 inch pizza.

8. Spread the tomato sauce onto the pizza and add the sliced beef.

9. Tear the mozzarella over the beef and cook in the oven for 6-7 minutes.

10. When the pizza is cooked and the dough is crispy, remove from the oven and finish with torn basil leaves and some grated Parmesan.

43

CHICKEN CURRY

 Prep time: 10 minutes   **Cook time:** 20 minutes   **Serves:** 4 people

1 onion, chopped

2 garlic cloves, roughly chopped

thumb-size fresh ginger, roughly chopped

4 tbsp korma paste

4 chicken breasts, cut into small chunks

50g ground almonds (optional)

4 tbsp sultanas

400ml chicken stock

1/4 tsp golden caster sugar

150g pot 0% fat free Greek yoghurt

small bunch coriander, chopped

320g brown basmati rice

1. Put the onion, garlic and ginger into a food processor and whizz to a paste. Alternatively, chop into very small pieces. Next, tip the paste into a large, high-sided pan with 3 tbsp water and cook for 5 minutes. Add the korma paste and cook for a further 2 minutes.

2. Stir the chicken into the sauce, add ground almonds, sultanas, stock and sugar. Give everything a good mix, cover and simmer for 10 minutes or until the chicken is cooked through.

3. While the chicken simmers, heat a large pan of boiling water and add the rice. Cover and simmer for 10-15 minutes or until cooked.

4. Serve with rice.

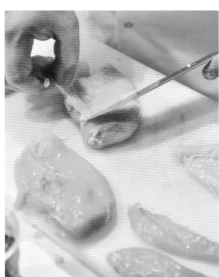

Emma & Cyrus Todiwala

TOAD IN THE HOLE
WITH CREAMY MASH AND PEAS

 Prep time: 40 minutes   **Cook time:** 35 minutes   **Serves:** 4 people

8 sausages

cooking oil

200g plain flour

3 eggs

300ml milk

splash of vinegar

pinch of salt & pepper

500g potatoes

50g butter

splash of milk

500g frozen peas

1. Preheat the oven to 190°C/Gas 5. Mix together the flour, milk, eggs, vinegar, salt and pepper in a bowl. Leave to stand for 20 minutes.

2. Peel and chop the potatoes. Put in a large saucepan of water, bring to the boil then lower to a simmer for 20 minutes.

3. Put small amount of oil in a baking tray. Prick the sausages then bake in the oven on the tray for 10 minutes.

4. Using individual Yorkshire pudding baking tins, place one sausage and a little oil into each hole, pour over the batter and place on the middle shelf of the oven. Turn the oven up to 220°C/Gas 8. Cook for 30 minutes.

5. Put a pan of water on to heat, and when it is simmering add frozen peas and cook for 5 minutes.

6. Drain the potatoes and mash with the butter and a little milk until smooth and creamy. Then stir in the drained, cooked peas.

7. Serve with the pudding on top of the mash.

CHICKEN KIEV

 Prep time: 35 minutes   **Cook time:** 25 minutes   **Serves:** 2 people

2 chicken supremes

a stick of garlic butter

100g panko bread crumbs

2 eggs, beaten

100g flour

200g mushrooms

100g pancetta

handful of button onions, or 1 small onion

100g white beans soaked and cooked in chicken stock

200ml chicken stock reduced to 4 tbsp of glaze

200ml double cream

handful of parsley

squeeze of lemon

1. Butterfly the chicken supremes and fill with garlic butter. Roll in cling film to form an oblong shape.

2. Secure tightly and place in the fridge at -2 degrees for 2 hours to firm up.

3. Put the eggs, flour and bread crumbs into three separate bowls.

4. Unwrap the chicken from cling film and then roll in flour, egg and bread crumbs twice to coat. Then place back in the fridge for 2 hours.

5. Deep fry the chicken at 180°C until golden – then place in a pre-heated oven at 200°C/Gas 6 degrees for 12 minutes.

6. For the mushrooms – sauté the pancetta in butter until brown then add the mushrooms and sauté until brown. Add the halved button onions and cook until golden. Drain, add the chicken glaze (reduced stock), cream, white beans, lemon and parsley, and simmer for 2 minutes.

7. Serve the sauce with the chicken kiev on top.

Shannon & Jolyon Yates

CHEESY BURGER BIRD NESTS

 Prep time: 30 minutes   **Cook time:** 15 minutes   **Serves:** 4 people

Beef Burgers:

1 small red onion, finely diced

1 tsp garlic powder

1 tsp salt and pepper

500g of lean mince

Cheese Sauce:

500ml chicken stock, reduced to 200ml

30ml dry sherry

120g grated Gruyère cheese

20g cornflour

20g soft cheese

knob of butter

Vegetable Mash:

1 onion, diced

garlic clove, crushed

1 large parsnip, peeled and diced

1 or 2 leeks, sliced and diced

300g-350g potatoes

1 tsp English mustard

60-80g soft cheese

salt and a knob of butter to taste

4 medium eggs

1 small broccoli

Beef Burger Method

This is stage 1: the burgers have to rest, giving you time to make the sauce and cook the vegetable mash.

1. Put the mince in a large bowl, sprinkle all the other burger ingredients on top and mix thoroughly until everything is evenly mixed.

2. Split into 4 patties, shape them so they are the same size and very flat (you are going to build a wall of mash round the edges forming a nest, so that gives you the idea of size).

3. Cover in cling film and place them in the fridge for 30 minutes to firm up.

4. You can also make batches of these ahead of time and freeze.

Cheesy Burger Bird Nests

Cheese Sauce Method

This is stage 2: The sauce re-heats really well in the microwave and keeps really well in the fridge, or you can leave it on a low heat when it's made. My mum makes this in batches and keeps it in the fridge to use for cauliflower cheese or macaroni cheese.

1. Reduce the chicken stock from 500ml to roughly 200ml.

2. Add the reduced stock and sherry to a pan over a medium heat, not boiling.

3. Mix in the grated Gruyère cheese and the cornflower and mix well until the cheese is incorporated into the stock.

4. Remove the pan from the heat and use as required.

Vegetable Mash Method

This is Stage 3: This vegetable mash is a great combination of potatoes, leeks, onions, broccoli carrots and parsnips, all mixed together to create a creamy delight. It can all be ready in a mere 20 minutes, but if you're really short of time, speed things up a bit by using ready prepared mashed potato.

1. Gently cook the diced onion, garlic, leeks and finely chopped broccoli heads with a few tbsps of salted water in a saucepan with the lid on for 5 minutes until the vegetables are tender (calorie friendly version) or soften them with butter and olive oil. You can add salt and butter to taste. Drain well.

2. Meanwhile boil the peeled potatoes and parsnip in salted water until tender. Drain, then mash with the milk, mustard and cream cheese, and add salt to taste.

3. Stir the drained onion, garlic, leek and broccoli into the mashed potato. This should be quite a stiff consistency (you are building walls with the potato so it needs to be robust).

Finally ...

Stage 4; construction and finishing off.

1. Preheat the oven to 200°C/ Gas 6. Take the patties from the fridge and place on a baking tray and, using the mash, construct a wall of mashed vegetable in a circle all the way round the outside of the burger (no holes).

2. When you have done all four, crack each egg, draining away some of the white using a slotted spoon, and place a raw egg into the centre of each of the nests.

3. Pop the tray in the oven for 15 minutes or until the eggs have set white on top (the yolks should be runny).

4. Serve immediately with the cheese sauce.

Elliot & Chris Lee

AMERICAN MEATBALLS WITH RICE

 Prep time: 20 minutes **Cook time:** 35 minutes **Serves:** 4 people

1. First put all your meatball ingredients into one bowl and mix well together with hands then put in some salt and pepper for seasoning.

2. Shape your meatballs by rolling small balls of the mixture in your hands. You should make 10-20, depending on the size.

3. For the tomato sauce, heat the oil on a low heat in a shallow pan with the lid off. Add the onion and garlic and sweat until they are translucent, stirring occasionally.

4. Add the tomato puree and chopped tomatoes. Once they are bubbling, add your meatballs. Reduce the heat and put the lid on and cook for 30 minutes, turning the meatballs occasionally.

5. Whilst your meatballs are cooking, put the rice and 700ml of water into a saucepan and cook on a medium heat.

6. Serve the meatballs and sauce on a bed of rice, garnish with parsley and serve immediately.

Meatballs:

3 slices of wholemeal bread, shredded into crumbs

650g fresh beef mince

1 onion, finely chopped

125ml tomato puree

1 egg, lightly beaten

salt and pepper

Sauce:

2 tbsp sunflower oil

1 onion, finely chopped

3 garlic cloves, finely chopped

2 tbsp tomato puree

1 can chopped tomatoes

Rice:

270g brown rice

chopped fresh parsley to garnish

Austin & John Woodward

CARAMELIZED ONION CHOP TOAD
WITH BASHED SQUASH AND PEAS

 Prep time: 45 minutes   **Cook time:** 35 minutes   **Serves:** 4 people

6 lamb cutlets

200g flour

3 eggs

100ml milk

1 onion

splash of oil

50g sugar

50g butter

½ butternut squash

200g peas

1 spring onion

seasoning

gravy

1. Preheat the oven to 200°C/ Gas 6. To make the bashed squash and peas, peel and cut the butternut squash into cubes. Roast the butternut squash in the oven for 25 to 30 minutes with a little butter and the thyme.

2. When the squash is cooked, blanch the peas and crush together – not too much, leave some texture. Season the peas and mix with the roast butternut squash. Turn the oven down to 160°C/Gas 3.

3. Peel and slice the onion and add to a large pan with a little oil, sugar and butter. Cook them slowly until they are soft and brown.

4. Make a Yorkshire pudding batter by mixing the flour and eggs then the milk, keep to one side.

5. Seal the lamb cutlets in a hot pan for a few minutes then add to a greased oven dish. Slice the spring onions then add to the dish with the lamb and cooled caramelized onions.

6. Pour in the batter mix and cook for 25 minutes until the batter and lamb is cooked.

7. Reheat the bashed squash and peas and serve piping hot with some gravy.

BEEF FIRE

 Prep time: 20 minutes   **Cook time:** 20 minutes   **Serves:** 4 people

400g beef

2 stalks of lemongrass

3 garlic cloves

1 or 2 hot chillis – depending on taste

splash of oil

salt

270g Thai rice

1. Slice the beef and marinate with ½ tsp powdered soup (optional) and season with some salt. Leave for 10 minutes to infuse.

2. Finely chop the lemongrass, chilli and garlic.

3. Put the sauté pan on a medium heat with a splash of oil. Cook the finely chopped garlic, chilli and lemongrass for a few minutes, until soft.

4. Next, add the beef and fry lightly so that the meat is lightly cooked – do not over cook.

5. The meat should be soft, not chewy or dry – the cooking time is very quick.

6. Add the rice to a pan of boiling water. Simmer for 10-15 minutes, or until cooked.

7. Serve with boiled Thai rice.

Neil & Eric Allouard

Corn Fed Chicken Cordon Bleu
with Vegetable Tagliatelle and Tarragon Jus

 Prep time: 45 minutes **Cook time:** 25 minutes **Serves:** 4 people

4 chicken breasts

1 egg

100g panko bread crumbs

50g plain flour

400ml milk

50g butter

100g diced cooked ham

150g Comté cheese

Vegetable tagliatelle:

3 carrots

1 red pepper

1 white onion

2 courgettes

¼ bunch parsley

50g butter

200ml chicken jus

½ bunch tarragon

1. Slice the chicken in half horizontally, nearly all the way through.

2. Bring the milk to boil then add the butter and flour, mix and cook for 5 minutes. Then add the cheese and ham. Season to taste.

3. Stuff the chicken with the cheese and ham sauce.

4. Put the egg into a bowl, beat lightly. Put the flour into another bowl, and the bread crumbs into another. Toss the chicken in the flour, then egg, then bread crumbs.

5. With a peeler shave the courgette and carrot.

6. Finely chop the red pepper and white onion.

7. Heat a pan, melt the butter and then add the shaved vegetables. Cook for five minutes on a medium heat.

8. In a fryer cook the chicken for 4 minutes and then place in an oven for 12 minutes at 180°C/ Gas 4.

9. Serve the chicken on top of the vegetables.

ROAST CHICKEN THIGHS
WITH SWEETCORN AND AVOCADO SALSA

 Prep time: 20 minutes   **Cook time:** 30 minutes   **Serves:** 6 people

12 small skin-on chicken thighs

4 garlic cloves

20g ginger, peeled

3 tbsp light soy sauce

1 tbsp dark soy sauce

½ tsp sesame oil

3 tbsp honey

2 x 165g cans salt free sweetcorn

2 ripe avocados, diced

20 cherry tomatoes, quartered

juice of 1 lime

1. Using a mini chopper or blender, blitz the garlic and ginger into a fine paste with 10 tsp water and 2 tsp vegetable oil.

2. Marinate the chicken with the ginger and garlic paste, light soy, dark soy, sesame oil and honey for at least ½ hour. If you marinate the chicken in the fridge, remove the chicken from the fridge 10 minutes before putting it in the oven.

3. Preheat the oven to 180°C/ Gas 4. Roast the chicken thighs for 30 minutes. Remove when cooked.

4. While the chicken cooks, mix together the salsa ingredients and serve with the chicken.

Ben & Chris Lee

PAELLA

 Prep time: 10 minutes　　 **Cook time:** 35 minutes　　**Serves:** 4 people

2 chicken breasts

1 onion

1 red or green pepper

2 tomatoes

100g chorizo, sliced

200g risotto rice

1 handful frozen peas

450ml vegetable stock

2 tsp turmeric

olive oil

salt and pepper to season

1. Roughly chop the chicken breasts. Chop the onion, pepper and tomatoes finely.

2. Heat a paella pan, or large, flat pan. Brown the chicken and onion in a dash of olive oil.

3. Add the pepper and tomatoes and simmer for 5 minutes.

4. Add the stock and risotto rice and bring to a simmer.

5. Add the turmeric and simmer for 25 minutes, stirring occasionally.

6. Add the peas and sliced chorizo.

7. Continue to simmer for a final five minutes.

8. Stir and season to taste before serving.

Ben & Chris Lee

HAM & EGGS

  Prep time: Overnight soaking, 8 hours slow cooking, 12 hours chilling

Cook time: 30-40 minutes **Serves:** 2 people

1 collar of ham (soaked in water for 24 hours)

apple juice – enough to cover ham in oven proof dish

1 kg of chopped onion, carrots, celery and leeks.

fresh rosemary and thyme, a few sprigs of each

2 bulbs of garlic – halved

4 bay leaves

2 duck eggs

200g baby spinach

butter

1. Place the ham in some water and leave to soak for 24 hours to remove the salt.

2. Drain the ham and put into a large oven proof dish with all the vegetables, herbs, garlic and cover with apple juice.

3. Cook at 110°C/Gas ¼ for 8 hours.

4. Remove the ham from the liquid and strain the liquid – discard the vegetables and herbs.

5. Reduce the cooking liquid by half by boiling rapidly.

6. Roll the ham tightly in cling film and chill for 12 – 24 hours.

7. Cut the ham into 6 – 8 oz portions.

8. Reheat the ham in the reduced cooking liquid until warmed through – approximately 20 minutes.

9. Sautè the spinach in butter until wilted – drain on kitchen paper.

10. To serve, place the spinach in the base of the bowl.

11. Place the ham on top – fry the duck egg in oil and butter and top the ham.

12. Serve with deep fried croquettes and mustard sauce.

VEGETARIAN

Leala & Aldo Zilli

ARANCINI WITH TALEGGIO

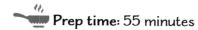 **Prep time:** 55 minutes    **Cook time:** 3 minutes    **Serves:** 4 people

500ml vegetable stock

40g coconut oil

1 ½ onions, finely chopped

4 cloves of garlic, finely chopped

250g Arborio or carnaroli rice

200ml white wine

handful of flat parsley leaves, roughly chopped

1 bunch of chives, finely chopped

1 bunch of mint leaves, finely chopped

55g vegetarian Parmesan-type cheese, finely grated, plus extra for serving

100g taleggio

100g coconut flour

2 eggs, lightly whisked

125g dry bread crumbs

coconut oil for deep frying

1 lemon, cut into wedges

1. Bring the stock to the boil in a large saucepan then maintain it at a gentle simmer.

2. Meanwhile, heat the 40g of coconut oil in a saucepan, on a medium to low heat, add the onions & garlic and cook till soft and translucent in colour.

3. **Tip.** Place some baking parchment & a lid over the onion mix, this helps the onions sweat down quicker and helps to deter burning.

4. Once the onion mix has softened, add the rice and cook for 2 minutes, mixing well and coating all the rice, then add the wine and simmer until evaporated.

5. Then, slowly, with one ladle at a time, add the hot stock to the rice mixture, stir continuously and allow to absorb before adding the next ladle. Keep repeating the process until all the stock has been used up, the rice mixture should be almost cooked. Stir the herbs and cheese into the mixture until combined.

6. Allow to cool slightly, then spread onto a tray and chill in the fridge for 2 hours.

7. To shape the arancini, roll tablespoons of the risotto into balls, pull off 1cm pieces of the taleggio and press into the centre of the balls, then re-roll to enclose the cheese into the centre of the ball.

8. Place the coconut flour, egg and bread crumbs into 3 separate bowls.

9. Lightly dust the arancini in the coconut flour, dip into the egg and then roll in the bread crumbs until evenly coated.

10. Fill a wok or deep saucepan one third full with coconut oil, allow to melt and heat to 180°C/ Gas 4.

11. Deep fry the arancini in batches, for 3 minutes at a time, turning constantly, until heated through and golden brown. Drain onto kitchen paper.

12. Serve with grated Parmesan and the lemon wedges and some baby leaves drizzled with balsamic vinegar and a little coconut oil (melted).

Emma & Cyrus Todiwala

EGG AND VEGETABLE FRIED RICE

 **Prep time:** 20 minutes 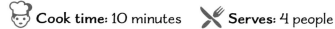 **Cook time:** 10 minutes  **Serves:** 4 people

500g boiled rice. The rice needs to be cold for this recipe so refrigerate after boiling

3 spring onions, sliced at a slant

1 green pepper, cut into fine strips. Use mixed if you like it to be more colourful. But no more than the equivalent of one pepper

mixed vegetables, blanched and cut small/diced. Or use shredded carrot, fine beans, diced mushrooms and green peas

2 eggs, well beaten

2 to 3 tbsp oil

salt, to taste

pepper powder, to taste. Use powder or finely crushed

soy sauce. A few dashes of either light or dark, but be careful if you use dark

1. Take a wok and add the oil.

2. Heat the oil to smoking point and allow to heat for a little while.

3. Add the beaten egg and swirl with the ladle or spoon, breaking it up as you go along.

4. Add the spring onions and the peppers and sauté for a minute, always keeping the heat high.

5. Add the vegetables, salt and pepper and sauté for a minute or so stirring, and tossing from time to time.

6. Add the rice and toss gently.

7. If you do not know how to toss with a wok, use the frying spoon.

8. Once the rice is heated through, season with salt and pepper and a dash, or a few dashes, of soy sauce. Taste and serve.

Jamie & Simon Wood

SPICY 'EVERYTHING' SOUP
WITH SODA BREAD

 Prep time: 20 minutes   **Cook time:** 2 ¼ Hours   **Serves:** 6 to 8 people

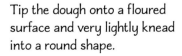

75g chorizo

2 medium carrots

2 leeks

3 sticks of celery

1 red pepper

1 vegetable stock cube

2 tsp paprika

1 tsp oregano

½ tsp thyme

½ tsp black pepper

45g dried spaghetti

1 courgette

2 tsp sugar

2 heaped tbsp tomato puree

2L water

500g soda bread flour

300ml buttermilk (approx)

1 egg

½ tsp salt

Bread

1. Heat the oven to 200°C/Gas 6. Place the flour and salt in large bowl. Mix the buttermilk and egg together and mix with a fork.

2. Add the buttermilk and egg to the flour and stir it all together with a fork. The dough should be quite wet/sticky.

3. Finish off the dough, mixing by hand.

4. If the mixture is too wet to handle add a little more flour.

Tip the dough onto a floured surface and very lightly knead into a round shape.

5. Place the dough on a baking sheet lined with baking paper. Score a deep cross on the top and dust lightly with flour. Place into the middle of the oven for 30 minutes until browned on top.

6. Remove your bread from the oven and allow to cool before slicing.

Soup

1. Chop the chorizo into small pieces (approx 1cm) and fry in a large pot until the oil is released then remove from the heat.

2. Chop the vegetables into bite-sized pieces. Add the leeks to the pot and sauté with the chorizo for 2 minutes. Then add all of the other vegetables, spices and herbs and stir.

3. Add the tomato puree, stock cube, sugar and water and bring to the boil. Finally, break up spaghetti strands into small pieces (approx 2cm) and add to the soup. Simmer for approx 30 minutes until the vegetables are soft.

Thuan & Kelly Snowdon
VEGETABLE SPRING ROLLS

 Prep time: 60 minutes   **Cook time:** 15 minutes   **Serves:** 4 people

40 medium size spring roll pastries

1 small tin of sweetcorn

1 small tin of green peas

2 carrots

small bunch of coriander

1 tbsp vegetarian oyster sauce

2 tsp sesame oil

1 tsp vegetable powder

vegetable oil

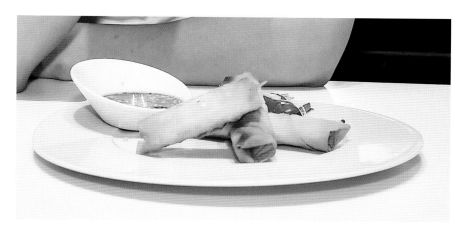

1. First, peel the carrots and wash them. After washing, chop them very small and mix in a bowl with the sweetcorn and peas.

2. In a bowl, mix the vegetarian oyster sauce and sesame oil, mix and leave to stand for 5 minutes.

3. Fill 1 spring onion pastry with 1 tablespoon of the vegetables. Use your fingertips to apply the oyster sauce and oil paste to the edge of the pastry.

4. Gently, but tightly, roll the spring roll. Seal the end with the paste and place with the sealed side down.

5. Spread some of the paste on the side of the spring roll and tuck the side in, pressing gently. Do the same with the other side.

6. Add 8 large cups of vegetable oil into a small pan and put on a high heat. When the oil is hot, put the spring rolls in to fry, 5-6 at a time. Once they are golden, turn them over and fry the other side.

7. Remove the spring rolls from the pan with a slotted spoon.

8. You can eat them with red chilli sauce or sweet chilli sauce.

QUICK MEALS & SIDES

SPANISH OMELETTE

 Prep time: 15–20 minutes   **Cook time:** 10–15 minutes   **Serves:** 2 people

2. When the egg starts to set, place the frying pan under the preheated grill. When the egg starts to cook you will see it start to rise. Add the prawns and cheese. Leave under the grill until brown then return to the hob.

3. Turn the omelette over in half and brown some more.

4. Serve with a mixed salad of rocket, olives, tomato, all chopped up with a balsamic vinegar dressing.

1 tbsp olive oil

1/4 small onion

1/4 yellow, red and green pepper

2 chestnut mushrooms

1 or 2 vine tomatoes

100g sweetcorn (tinned)

40-50g strong cheese, grated

10 cooked king prawns

4 eggs, whisked

salt & pepper

1. Preheat the grill to a medium heat. Take the four eggs and whisk together. Then chop the onion, peppers and mushrooms and put everything into a frying pan and fry the above until soft. When soft, add vine tomatoes and sweetcorn.

Isobel & Wayne Sleep
TYPICAL CORNISH PASTY

 Prep time: 40 minutes   **Cook time:** 45 minutes   **Serves:** 2 people

225g self-raising flour

115g lard

pinch of salt

water

225g beef skirt, cut into small cubes

2 to 3 large potatoes

1 piece turnip or swede

1 onion, peeled and chopped

salt and pepper

1. Sift the flour with the salt, rub in the fat, and mix to a pliable consistency with some water. Leave to rest for half an hour.

2. Split the pastry in half and cut out two circles about 5mm thick.

3. Peel and slice the potatoes thinly into the centre of both circles to form a base for the rest of the filling.

4. Slice the turnip thinly over the potato, then spread the beef on top.

5. Add a little onion, season with salt and pepper.

6. Dampen the edge of the circle of pastry with water to help seal it. Bring together the edges to make a parcel with the filling in the centre.

7. There should be a neat parcel with the filling in the centre – make the pastry neater by crimping the edges. Fold over the edge to make it slightly thicker, then squeeze every 2cms to make a neat pattern along the edge.

8. Put the pasty on a piece of buttered paper, make a small slit on top to let the steam out, brush the top with a little milk, and put on a greased baking tray.

9. Bake it in a preheated over at 200°C/Gas 6 for 30 minutes, reduce the heat to 190°C/Gas 5 and cook for another 30 minutes.

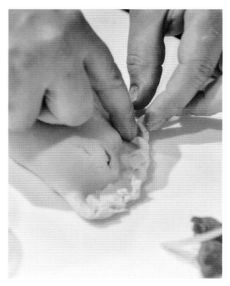

Leo & Tom Dell

Le Omelette

 Prep time: 20 minutes   **Cook time:** 5 minutes **Serves:** 1-2 people

3 eggs

1 tbsp milk

salt and pepper

½ courgette

3 slices of ham

1 bell pepper

75g cheese

1. Mix the eggs, milk, and a pinch of salt and pepper in a bowl.

2. Chop up the courgette, ham and bell pepper. Grate the cheese.

3. Put a large pan on to heat. Quickly pour in the egg mixture and top with the chopped ingredients.

4. When the egg starts to set, place under a medium grill until cooked.

5. Alternatively, half-fill cupcake cakes with the egg mixture and chopped ingredients. Bake in the oven at 200°C/Gas 6 for 10 minutes. Enjoy!

Sanna & Jamian Lewis

Aloo Paratha and Yoghurt

 Prep time: 30 minutes **Cook time:** 15 minutes **Serves:** 8-10 people

5-6 medium potatoes

¼ tsp salt

50g garam masala

50g fenugreek

1-2 medium onions, diced

3 chillies

50g ginger, peeled and chopped

oil

200g atta flour

water

1. Grind the onions and ginger together.

2. Prick the potatoes all over and microwave for 10 minutes.

3. Grind the chillies in a pestle and mortar.

4. After the potatoes are cooked, peel, chop and mash them, then mix all the ingredients together by hand.

5. Get a flat plan and put on a low heat.

6. Mix the atta flour with some water until it forms a soft dough. If it is dry, add some more water.

7. Roll a little ball of the atta dough and flatten a little.

8. Put a little of the potato mixture into the middle of the dough ball then fold or close up the ball so that the mixture can't come out.

9. Then roll out the dough until medium size. If it gets sticky then add some atta and carry on. It's like making a chappati but with a mixture.

10. Add oil on each side of the paratha and add to the hot pan. Keep flipping it while cooking as it cooks quickly.

11. Serve on a plate with a yoghurt dip.

Naht & Michiel Boereboom
SCOTCH EGGS

 Prep time: 50 minutes   **Cook time:** 8 minutes   **Serves:** 10 portions

10 eggs

1 kg sausage meat

300g plain flour

600g bread crumbs

2 eggs whisked

1. Boil 10 of the eggs for 4 minutes. Let them cool then peel.

2. Cover each egg with a thin layer of sausage meat, about 3mm thick.

3. Whisk the 2 remaining eggs and place in a bowl. Place the flour in a bowl, and the bread crumbs in another.

4. Pass the eggs though the flour, then the whisked eggs, and finally the bread crumbs.

5. Keep refrigerated and then fry when needed in a deep frier for 8 minutes.

6. **Tip:** Add salt and vinegar to the water when boiling the eggs. Leave them overnight in the water to cool – the salt and vinegar will make them much easier to peel.

Bethany & Sophie Thompson

FLATBREADS

 Prep time: 50 minutes   **Cook time:** 20 minutes   **Serves:** 10 servings

500g self-raising flour (gluten free)

salt and pepper

500g strained Greek yoghurt

100g herbs, can be dried ones or fresh thyme

50g turmeric (optional)

1. Mix all of the ingredients in a bowl until it forms a dough. You can cook the breads straight away or leave the dough to stand for about half an hour.

2. Make the dough into small balls. Roll/flatten the balls out into discs.

3. Griddle each flatbread on a dry griddle for approximately 2 minutes on each side. Serve sprinked with some herbs.

PASTA

Pasta with Cream, Ham and Peas

 Prep time: 25 minutes **Cook time:** 15 minutes **Serves:** 4 people

240g pasta

1 shallot, finely chopped

30ml extra virgin olive oil

100ml single cream

50g grated Parmesan

200g peas (either fresh in season, of petit pois frozen)

100g ½ cm thick cooked ham (York ham is fine or any good quality ham) cut in very small cubes or finely chopped.

1 tbsp chopped parsley

pinch of salt

1. In a shallow pan add the extra virgin olive oil and the finely chopped shallot and sauté until soft.

2. In the meantime, in a small pan, cook the fresh or frozen peas, drain and set aside.

3. Add the finely chopped ham to the shallot and cook gently for a couple of minutes.

4. At this stage add the peas, and season to taste but be aware the ham is already salted and Parmesan will be added eventually.

5. When all ingredients are well incorporated, add the cream and warm through.

6. In the meantime boil a copious amount of water (at least one litre per 100g of pasta), and when boiling add the salt, roughly 2 tbsp rock salt, then add the pasta.

7. Cook to al dente (approx. 12 minutes).

8. Drain the pasta well and add it to the sauce, mix well and sprinkle with the chopped parsley and the Parmesan. Serve at once.

Jacob & Kelly Snowdon

SPAGHETTI VONGOLE

 **Prep time:** 15 minutes **Cook time:** 15 minutes **Serves:** 4 people

200g mussels

500g prawns

200g squid

1 large bunch fresh coriander

4 garlic cloves

10 cherry tomatoes

50ml white wine vinegar

400g dried spaghetti

sea salt

freshly ground black pepper

extra virgin olive oil

1-2 dried chillies

2 vegetable stock cubes

1. Put a pan of water on to boil. Rinse the seafood with warm water.

2. Put a large pan with a lid on a high heat and let it heat up. Finely slice the coriander stalks, then put them to one side and roughly chop the leaves.

3. Peel and chop the garlic, quarter the tomatoes and get your wine vinegar ready.

4. Add the pasta to the boiling water with a good pinch of salt and cook until al dente. About 5 minutes before the pasta is ready, get ready to start cooking – you'll have to be quick.

5. Put 4 generous lugs of extra virgin olive oil into the hot pan and add the garlic, coriander stalks, the squid and a good pinch of salt and pepper. Crumble in the dried chilli and add the chopped tomatoes. Stir everything around constantly and, just as the garlic starts to colour, tip in the seafood and pour in the wine vinegar. It will splutter and steam, so give everything a good shake and put the lid on the pan.

6. After about 3 or 4 minutes shuffle the pan around.

7. Take the pan off the heat. By now your pasta should be just about perfect.

8. Drain and add the prawns to the pan along with the coriander leaves and an extra drizzle of extra virgin olive oil.

9. Stir or toss for a further minute or two to let the beautiful seashore juices from the mussels be absorbed into the pasta.

10. Serve right away with some fresh hunks of bread to mop up the juices. Beautiful!

HANDMADE TAGLIATELLE
WITH FRESH TOMATOES AND SPINACH

 Prep time: 25 minutes   **Cook time:** 20 minutes   **Serves:** 2-4 people

To make pasta:

300g 00 pasta flour

3-4 eggs

splash of olive oil

dessert spoon of salt for the pasta boiling water

OR

300g fresh egg tagliatelle

Other ingredients:

olive oil

salt

freshly grated Parmesan cheese

freshly ground black pepper

chopped parsley and basil for garnish

100g fresh spinach leaves

300g fresh sun-ripened tomatoes

1 garlic clove, finely chopped

olive oil

dried chilli flakes (optional)

dried oregano

salt and pepper

The pasta

1. Place the flour on a worktop (or in a large bowl) and make a well in the centre. Whisk together the eggs and olive oil and pour into the well, working the flour into the eggs. Keep working until you have achieved an homogenous lump then begin to knead with the heel of your hand. Continue kneading until you have achieved a soft, silky texture throughout. Wrap in plastic film and refrigerate for 15 minutes before continuing with your recipe.

2. For pappardelle or tagliatelle, roll out the pasta on a lightly floured surface using a rolling pin until thin enough to see the grain of the table through the sheet of pasta. Dust with flour again, roll up and cut with a knife to the required thickness.

HANDMADE TAGLIATELLE
WITH FRESH TOMATOES AND SPINACH

Shake out to unravel and hang up to dry for an hour or so before boiling in plenty of salted water for about a minute to achieve an 'al dente' texture. Drain and serve tossed into your favourite sauce.

3. For best results use a pasta rolling machine. The above is the traditional hand-made method, for quicker results place the flour, eggs and olive oil into a processor and pulse for a few seconds. Turn out onto a work surface and pull the dough together. Wrap and chill in the same way. Then roll out to about 1-inch thick and pass through a pasta rolling machine.

The sauce

1. Cut large tomatoes into quarters, medium in half and leave small ones whole.

2. Place in an ovenproof dish with the chopped garlic, salt, pepper and oregano, plus chilli flakes, if using.

3. Pour over a generous quantity of olive oil and toss all about.

4. Place in a hot oven, 200°C/Gas 6, for approx. 15 minutes until well cooked and browned at the edges.

5. Wilt the spinach in a dry non-stick pan, season with salt and pepper.

6. Cook the tagliatelle in plenty of boiling, salted water for just 1 minute.

7. Put the cooked tomatoes into a large bowl and stir through the cooked spinach.

8. Transfer the cooked tagliatelle to the tomatoes and spinach and stir through – you may need to add a little of the pasta cooking water to loosen the mixture.

9. Serve in warmed bowls with a sprinkling of chopped parsley and basil, grated Parmesan and a twist of black pepper.

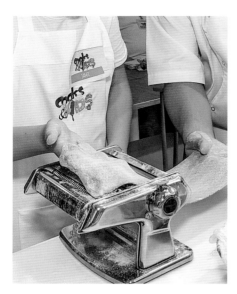

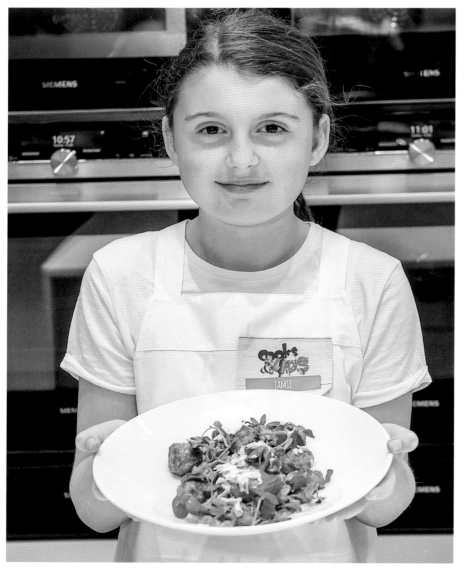

Jamie & Simon Wood

Tagliatelle Verde with Pork and Herb Mascarpone Meatballs

 Prep time: 40 minutes **Cook time:** 25 minutes **Serves:** 4 people

For the meatballs:

300g pork mince

300g beef mince

1 tsp dried oregano

1 tbsp fresh oregano, chopped

50g bread crumbs

75g ricotta

sea salt and white pepper

For the pasta:

300g 00 pasta flour

3 free range eggs

iced water

75g cooked spinach

For the pesto:

50g pine nuts

2 garlic cloves

2 large bunches of basil

50g Parmesan

150ml olive oil

juice of ½ a lemon

handful of peashoots

1. Fill a large saucepan with water, season well, and bring it to the boil. Add in the spinach leaves and cook for 20-30 seconds, then immediately put into the iced water to stop the cooking process. Stir it around to ensure even cooking. When cool, remove from the water, squeeze in a towel until dry and then place in the bowl of a food processor and puree until a very fine paste forms.

2. Next, add in 3 eggs and blend, then add in the flour and blitz it up until it resembles a crumble. Remember, it's not exact and you may need to add a little more egg or flour to get the consistency.

3. Empty the crumble out onto a floured work surface and bring it together with your hands, knead it for a couple of minutes to activate the gluten, roll it into a ball and cover in film to rest for around 15 minutes.

4. Next, roll out the pasta on a lightly floured surface using a rolling pin until thin enough to see the grain of the table through the sheet of pasta. Dust with flour again, roll up and cut with a knife to the required thickness. Shake out to unravel and hang up to dry for an hour or so before boiling in plenty of salted water for about a minute to achieve an 'al dente' texture.

5. For your meatballs, combine all of the ingredients into a large mixing bowl, use a large serving spoon to mix well and then, using wet hands, roll them onto balls.

6. Add a little olive oil to a large frying pan followed by the meatballs and gently fry until browned, and cooked through, around 10 – 12 minutes. Drain off any excess fat and leave to rest for 3 or 4 minutes.

7. For the pesto, take the basil, garlic, pine nuts, olive oil, juice of the lemon and ¾ of the Parmesan and blend to a paste and season.

8. Next, in a frying pan, add some olive oil and 2 tablespoons of pesto per person, add in your pasta and combine well. Top with the meatballs and a generous shaving of Parmesan and peashoots.

Neil & Eric Allouard

MACARONI SURPRISE

 Prep time: 30 minutes   **Cook time:** 15-20 minutes   **Serves:** 4 people

5. Add the mustard and half of the cheese.

6. Drain the macaroni. Add the sauce to the macaroni. Get a large dish and put the leek and the bacon in the bottom. Pour over the saucy macaroni. Put the rest of the cheese on the top.

7. Put in the oven at 180°C/Gas 4 for 15-20 minutes.

8. Serve with crusty bread and butter.

350g macaroni

salt

350ml of milk

25g butter

1 tbsp plain flour

110g grated cheese

1/4 tsp wholegrain mustard

1 packet bacon

1 large leek

1 tbsp oil

1/4 tsp oregano

1/4 tsp garlic

1/4 tsp turmeric

1. Cut the bacon into squares. Slice the leek. Gently fry them together with a little oil and turmeric.

2. Fill a large pan with boiling water and a little salt. Boil the macaroni for 10 minutes or until ready.

3. Melt the butter in a saucepan. Take off the heat when melted. Add the flour until it leaves the side of the pan. Add the milk, a little at a time, until it is smooth.

4. Gently bring the sauce to the boil. Then turn it down and let it simmer for a few minutes on a very low heat.

PESTO PASTA

 Prep time: 40 minutes   **Cook time:** 10 minutes   **Serves:** 4 people

Pesto

½ garlic clove

pinch of sea salt

pinch of ground black pepper

3 handfuls of fresh basil leaves

1 handful of pine nuts (toasted in a frying pan)

1 large handful of Parmesan cheese (grated)

extra virgin olive oil

a small squeeze of a lemon (if you want to)

handful of chestnut mushrooms – chopped

Italian unsmoked pancetta

Pasta

fresh spaghetti pasta made with fresh egg

1. In a food processor put the garlic, salt, pepper and basil leaves and blend them together.

2. Once blended, add the pine nuts to the mixture and blend.

3. Remove the mixture from the food processor and put it into a bowl. Then add half of the Parmesan cheese, stir together gently and add olive oil. Add just enough olive oil for the mixture to bind together to make an oozy consistency.

4. Then add the remaining Parmesan cheese and oil until you get the consistency and taste that you are happy with. You can add a squeeze of lemon to add a nice zesty twang if you want to.

5. In a frying pan, add the pancetta (no oil) and fry for 2 minutes then add the mushrooms and fry for a further 1 minute. Once these are cooked put to the side until needed.

6. Fill a large saucepan half full with water, add a pinch of salt and a dash of olive oil to the water and bring to the boil. Add the pasta and simmer for 4 minutes.

7. Once the pasta is cooked drain and place in a large dish. Add the Pancetta and mushrooms to the pasta, then the pesto mixture and mix altogether. Serve and enjoy.

PASTA SURPRISE

 Prep time: 10 minutes   **Cook time:** 25 minutes   **Serves:** 4 people

300g fusilli pasta swirls

4 rashers of unsmoked back bacon

1 onion

1 pepper (red or green)

2 tomatoes

4 mushrooms

50g salted butter

2 tbsp plain flour

450ml milk

100g mature cheddar cheese, grated

salt and pepper to season

1. Chop the bacon, onion, pepper, mushrooms and tomatoes finely.

2. Heat a pan with a splash of olive oil. Add the onion and bacon and soften for 5 minutes.

3. Add the mushrooms, tomatoes and pepper and cook for 3 minutes. Set aside.

4. Melt the butter in a pan then add the flour and mix until smooth. Cook for 2 minutes to make a roux.

5. Take the butter and flour off the heat and gradually add the milk, stirring constantly.

6. Put the pan back on the heat and bring to the boil.

7. Remove the pan from the heat and add the cheese. Season to taste.

8. Add the cooked vegetables and bacon to the cheese sauce and mix.

9. Set the sauce to one side, keeping warm on a low heat or in a covered bowl.

10. Boil a pan of water and cook the pasta according to the packet instructions.

11. When the pasta is cooked, drain and add to the cheese sauce.

12. Mix together and season to taste before serving.

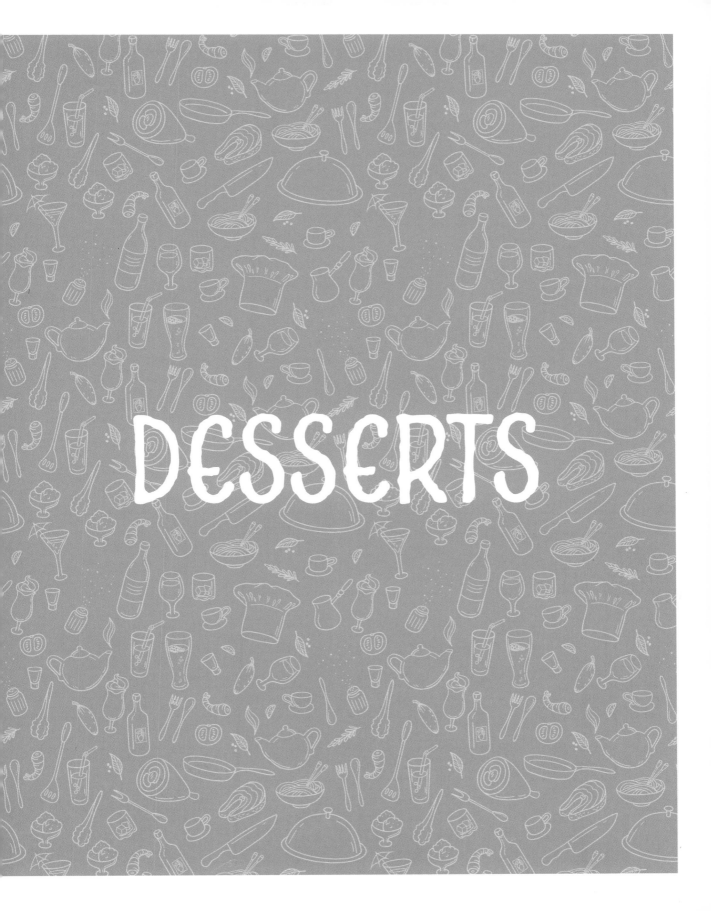

DESSERTS

Zahra & Tom Kerridge

STRAWBERRY CHEESECAKE

 Prep time: 45 to 50 minutes **Cook time:** 3 hours ✕ **Serves:** 6 to 8 people

75g melted butter

175g digestive biscuits, crushed

1 tbsp of gelatine (1 pack)

4 tbsp of warm water (for gelatine)

227g cream cheese

14-16 fresh strawberries, blended

75g caster sugar

142g double cream, lightly whipped

1. Combine the butter and biscuit crumbs. Press the mixture onto the base of an 8-inch round, loose bottom, spring form cake tin. Chill in the freezer while preparing the filling.

2. Place the gelatine in a small pan with the water and heat gently to dissolve, as per the instructions on the packet.

3. Beat the cream cheese until soft, and then stir in the blended strawberries, sugar and gelatine. Fold in the cream.

4. Spoon the mixture onto the biscuit base, level the surface and chill until set.

5. Transfer the cheesecake to a serving plate and add topping of your choice.

CHOCOLATE FONDANT

Prep time: 25 minutes **Cook time:** 8 minutes **Serves:** 6 people

continue to fold until nice and even.

4. Divide the mixture between the 6 ramekins and chill for around an hour. About 45 minutes into their chilling time, preheat the oven to 210°C/Gas 7.

5. Cook for 6-8 minutes until the tops resemble biscuits and are just beginning to crack.

6. Serve warm in the ramekins, garnished with some raspberries or strawberries.

100g dark chocolate

10g cocoa

100g butter

2 eggs

70g caster sugar

50g flour

½ tsp baking powder

raspberries or strawberries to garnish

1. Lightly butter 6 ramekins.

2. Fill a large saucepan half full with water, then place a small saucepan with the chocolate inside into the pan with water. Heat gently on the stovetop. When the chocolate melts, add the butter then remove from the heat and mix well together.

3. Whisk together the eggs and sugar in a bowl. Once the mixture is pale, creamy and fluffy, fold into the chocolate. Add the flour, cocoa and baking powder and

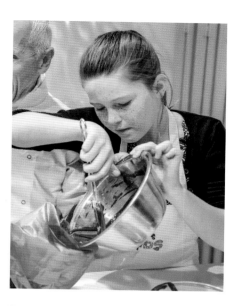

Sarah & Kelly Snowdon

SWEET STRAWBERRY SURPRISE

 Prep time: 1 hour   **Cook time:** 20–25 minutes   **Serves:** 8 people

For the sponge:

100g white chocolate

200g unsalted butter

3 large free range eggs

150g caster sugar

grated zest of ½ a lemon

200g self-raising flour

Fillings and topping:

1 punnet of strawberries

200ml double cream, whipped

2 grated cubes of dairy chocolate

5 bay leaves

50g white chocolate, melted

1. Preheat the oven to 180°C/ Gas 4.

2. Put the broken up white chocolate in to a microwave safe bowl then microwave it for 10 seconds and repeat until creamy. Add the butter and stir until melted.

3. Then put the eggs into a mixing bowl and whisk until frothy. Add the sugar and lemon zest and whisk it on high speed until it looks like mousse (approx 4 minutes).

4. Stir the chocolate and the eggy mixture together for a short time.

5. Sift the flour into the mixture then fold it using a metal spoon, do this very slowly.

6. Separate the mixture between two 25cm sandwich tins, making sure it is even. Bake for 20 to 25 minutes or until the cakes are light and golden.

7. When the cakes are out of the oven let them cool completely.

8. Then whip the cream and divide half of the cream between the two cakes. Spread onto the top of one cake, layer some strawberries on then flip the other cake on top like a sandwich.

9. Spread the other half of the cream on top of the cake and add the rest of your strawberries.

10. To make the leaf decoration, put some olive oil on a bay leaf and coat with a layer of melted white chocolate. Leave for 3-4 minutes and peel off the chocolate.

11. To finish, grate some milk chocolate over the top of your cake. Eat and enjoy!

Isobel & Wayne Sleep

SUGAR FREE TRIFLE

 **Prep time:** 2 hours   **Cook time:** 1 hour   **Serves:** 4 people

50g margarine

50g sweetener

50g self-raising flour

1 egg

packet of instant custard

250ml cream

450ml of mashed strawberries

100g of strawberries (for decoration)

Jelly:

150ml water

250g packet of sugar free jelly

1. Preheat the oven to 200°C/ Gas 6. Mix your strawberries in a small pan, on a low heat, with 100ml of water and mix until it's a mash.

2. Whilst this cooks, put your margarine, sweetener, self-raising flour and egg in a bowl and mix until smooth. Spread it out in a baking tray and bake in the oven for 10 minutes.

3. Cut the cooked sponge into 3cm chunks and place in your trifle bowl.

4. Prepare the jelly according to the packet instructions, but with only 150ml of water. Pour it on top of your cake and put in the fridge for 2-3 hours, or until set.

5. When your jelly is set, make your custard using the recipe on the packet. Put it into the fridge until your custard is firm enough to hold the cream. Then spoon it on top of your jelly.

6. Whip the cream until you can drag your mixer across and it leaves a trail in the bowl. Delicately place the cream on top of the custard and add some more strawberries for decoration.

Nia & Michel Roux Jr

LEMON PANCAKE GATEAU

 Prep time: 20 minutes   **Cook time:** 20 minutes   **Serves:** 4-6 people

2 eggs

125g white flour

80g wholemeal flour

500ml milk

pinch of salt

grated zest of 2 lemons

vegetable oil

fresh berries, to serve

Lemon butter:

3 eggs

juice and grated zest of 3 lemons

160g caster sugar

75g butter

1. To make the pancakes, mix the eggs into the flours with a whisk, then add the milk gradually to avoid any lumps. Finally, mix in the salt and lemon zest and leave the batter to rest for 1 hour.

2. Add a smear of vegetable oil to a non-stick pan and cook the pancakes. They should be very thin and well cooked, almost dry.

3. Preheat the oven to 200°C/ Gas 6. Line the base of a round, non-stick cake tin, about the same diameter as the pancakes, with greaseproof paper. Place a pancake in the tin followed by a thin layer of the lemon butter. Repeat the layers until all the pancakes and lemon butter

have been used. Cover with greaseproof paper and bake in the oven for 20 minutes. Leave to cool in the tin, then cut into slices when cold and serve with fresh berries. If you like, decorate with mint and orange zest.

Lemon butter

Whisk the eggs, sugar, lemon juice and zest together in a saucepan. Place over a medium heat and stir continuously until the mixture thickens. Do not boil. Pass the mixture through a fine sieve, then whisk in the butter, cut into small pieces. Cover and leave to cool.

Elliot & Sarah Danesin Medio
APPLE AND PEAR CRUMBLE

 Prep time: 25 minutes   **Cook time:** 40 minutes   **Serves:** 6 people

4. Place in the centre of the oven for approx 40 minutes until light brown. Cool when cooked.

5. Serve with double cream, custard or fromage frais.

4 bramley apples

4 large pears

30g sultanas

1 tsp cinnamon

3 tbsp honey

Crumble mix

200g plain flour

150g margarine or butter

150g demerara sugar or caster sugar

1. Preheat the oven to 180°C/ Gas 4. Chop the margarine into lumps and add it to a bowl with the flour. Rub together until they form the texture of fine bread crumbs. Add the sugar and lightly rub into the crumb.

2. Peel, core and chop the apples and pears. Put into a mixing bowl and pour over the honey and cinnamon. Rub the honey and cinnamon onto the fruit.

3. Place the fruit into a large oven dish and spread over the crumb mixture until all the fruit is covered.

BANOFFEE PIE

Prep time: 20 minutes　　**Cook time:** 2 ¼ hours　　**Serves:** 6 to 8 people

800ml condensed sweetened milk

6 tbsp melted butter plus extra for greasing

150g chocolate digestives, crushed plus 6 full

50g ground almonds

4 ripe bananas

1 tbsp of lemon juice

1 tbsp of vanilla essence

good quality chocolate to grate

450ml thick double cream whipped

1. Boil the condensed milk in a saucepan for 2 hours then leave to cool. Preheat the oven to 180°C/ Gas 4. Grease a 9 inch loose bottomed cake tin with butter.

2. Mix the butter, crushed biscuits and nuts together in a bowl. Transfer to the cake tin and press down onto the base. Place the remaining full biscuits in a circle in the tin, bake for 12 minutes and leave to cool.

3. Slice the bananas into a bowl and sprinkle the vanilla essence and lemon juice over the bananas then mix gently.

4. Add the banana mixture to the biscuit crust. Then spoon over the cooled condensed milk.

5. Whip the cream and spread over the cooled condensed milk before adding grated chocolate.

Baked Raspberry Cheesecake

Austin & John Woodward

Prep time: 15 minutes   **Cook time:** 20 minutes   **Serves:** 6 to 8 people

4. Crush the raspberries through a sieve and stir in the icing sugar. Spoon the raspberry juice on top of the cheesecake in patches – blobbing in small patches. Using a skewer or small palette knife, gently swirl through the raspberry patches to make a marble effect.

5. Bake in a preheated oven until the cake is a bit wobbly in the centre but not liquid, 20 to 30 minutes. Leave to stand for 20 minutes, then chill in the fridge for at least 6-8 hours or overnight.

85g butter

200g digestive biscuits, crushed

400g cream cheese

2 large eggs

1 tsp vanilla essence

1 punnet raspberries

3 tbsp icing sugar

1. Preheat the oven to 190°C/ Gas 5. Brush a 20cm (8") spring form tin with oil.

2. Melt the butter and add the crushed biscuits, stirring until completely coated in butter. Spread the biscuits over the bottom of the tin, pressing down with your knuckles to check it is firmly covering the surface.

3. Beat the cream cheese, eggs, sugar and vanilla essence in a large bowl until smooth. Pour over the bottom of the tin and smooth the top. Place the tin on a baking tray.

Georgia & Hannah Miles

SURPRISE-INSIDE FRENCH TOAST

 Prep time: 20 minutes　　 **Cook time:** 25 minutes　　 **Serves:** 4 portions

For the French toast:

1 brioche loaf

4 eggs

120ml double cream

2 tbsp caster sugar

1 tsp ground cinnamon (optional)

1 tsp vanilla bean powder (optional)

1–2 tablespoons butter, for frying

4 tbsp chopped salted peanuts, finely chopped (optional)

icing sugar, to dust

For the surprise fillings:

peanut butter

raspberry jam

white chocolate chips

dark chocolate chips

fresh raspberries

chocolate spread

ripe banana

1. Using a sharp knife, carefully cut a pocket in the top of 4 thick slices of brioche to create a large cavity. Take care not to cut all the way through as it is this cavity which will hold your filling.

2. Next fill the pockets with fillings of your choosing – such as peanut butter, jam and slices of banana or fresh raspberries and chocolate chips. Don't put too much filling in otherwise it will leak when you cook it. Press the bread down with your hand gently to seal the filling in.

3. Whisk together the eggs, cream and caster sugar in a mixing bowl, transfer to a shallow dish and set aside. Whisk in a little ground cinnamon or vanilla, if you wish. Melt the butter in a large frying pan and set over a medium heat until the butter begins to foam. Soak each slice in the egg mixture on one side for a few seconds, then turn over and soak the other side. The bread should be fully coated in egg, but not too soggy – it is best to soak one slice at a time. Put each slice straight in the pan before soaking and cooking the next. If you want to add a nut crumb, press one side of the soaked bread into the chopped peanuts and sprinkle with a little sugar.

4. Cook for 2–3 minutes on each side until the egg is cooked and the slice is golden brown. Keep the cooked toast warm while you cook the remaining slices in the same way, adding a little butter to the pan each time, if required.

5. Serve immediately, dusted with icing sugar.

Bethany & Sophie Thompson

CHOCOLATE CHEESECAKE

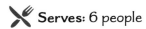 **Prep time:** 30 minutes   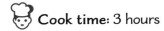 **Cook time:** 3 hours   **Serves:** 6 people

1kg mini chocolates, we use Heroes

150g digestive biscuits

75g unsalted butter (melted)

300ml double cream

70g icing sugar

juice of ½ lemon

280g cream cheese

1. Sort the chocolates, set aside some caramel chocolates and milk chocolates – we do Eclairs and Dairy Milk. Put the other chocolates in the fridge. Put the digestive biscuits in a bag and crush using a rolling pin and set aside.

2. Unwrap the caramel chocolates – e.g. Eclairs and put in a bowl. Add butter and microwave for 45 seconds. Add the biscuit crumbs and mix, then press into a loose bottom, spring form cake tin and put in the fridge.

3. Sort the chocolates again and place one of each back into the fridge. Chop each remaining chocolate in half and set aside.

4. Put the cream in a bowl and whip to soft peaks. Add in the icing sugar, cream cheese, lemon juice and the chopped chocolates. Mix gently then spoon over the base. Put it in the fridge overnight.

5. To serve, remove the cheesecake from the tin. Melt the remaining chocolates – e.g. Dairy Milk, and use a spoon to drizzle over the top. Decorate with the remaining chocolates.

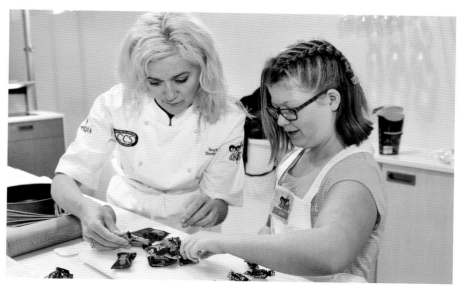

Naht & Michiel Boereboom
Baked Ricotta Cheesecake

 Prep time: 25 minutes **Cook time:** 40 minutes **Serves:** 8 people

8 digestive biscuits

50g butter

600g ricotta cheese

2 tbsp flour

175g sugar

vanilla extract

2 eggs + 1 yolk

142g sour cream

300g raspberries

1. Preheat the oven to 180°C/ Gas 4. Crush the biscuits into a bowl and mix with the butter until the mixture is smooth. Press into the bottom of a 20cm spring form, loose bottom cake tin. Bake for 5 minutes.

2. Mix the remaining ingredients together in a bowl. When the base is baked, pour the mixture on top of the base and bake in the oven for 40 minutes until it is wobbly.

3. Remove from the oven to cool down and top with some raspberries.

SWEET TREATS

Lucy & John Woodward

Scrummy Chocolate Treats

Prep time: 35 minutes   **Cook time:** 10-15 minutes   **Serves:** 6-12 portions

250g of wholegrain oat cereal (Cheerios are our favourite)

a packet of large marshmallows

golden syrup

100g dark chocolate

1. Break the chocolate into a measuring jug. Then put it in the microwave for 10 seconds, repeating until fully melted, being careful not to overcook the chocolate.

2. Get the cereal and mix it with the melted chocolate. Stir the mixture with a tablespoon till all of the cereal is covered in chocolate.

3. Once the mixture is completely coated in chocolate, use half of it to fill 4 cupcake cases.

4. Be sure to spread the mixture evenly – and reserve half as we need it for the top.

5. After the mixture has cooled down, cut up the marshmallows into fours. Put the marshmallow pieces into the cupcake cases making an interesting pattern.

6. With the rest of the cereal mixture, put another even layer on top of the marshmallows.

7. Finally, to give this treat a pop of sweetness drizzle a lot of golden syrup over each treat. If you would like to have this treat hard, then pop into the fridge.

GINGER AND LIME CAKE

 Prep time: 1.5 hours   **Cook time:** 17 minutes   **Serves:** 8 people

6. Stir until combined – DO NOT OVER MIX!

7. Spoon your mixture into your prepared tins.

8. Bake in your preheated oven for 17 minutes or until firm to touch and cooked in centre. You can check with a sharp knife, it should come out clean.

9. When cooked, leave to cool.

10. Once the cake is cool you can start with your icing.

11. Mix your cream cheese, icing sugar and lime juice until smooth and creamy.

12. Cover the top of one of the cakes with your icing or, alternatively, you can make a buttercream with lime juice in. Then sandwich the two cakes together and cover the top of the cake with your icing and lime rind – maybe adding some sliced strawberries and grapes to decorate.

280g plain flour

1 tbsp baking powder

1 ½ tsp ground ginger

pinch of salt

115g light brown sugar

2 eggs

250ml milk

85g butter, melted and cooled

1 tsp vanilla extract

1 ½ lime rind

Icing:

150g cream cheese

juice of 1 lime

200g icing sugar

rind of ½ lime, to decorate

1. Preheat the oven to 180°C/ Gas 4.

2. Grease and prepare two 8 inch cake tins.

3. Sift together the flour, baking powder, ginger and salt. Stir in the sugar.

4. Lightly beat your eggs in a large bowl then beat in your milk, butter, vanilla extract and lime rind.

5. Make a well in your dry ingredients and pour in your beaten liquid ingredients.

Kelsie & Sara Danesin Medio
RAINBOW CAKES

 Prep time: 40 minutes   **Cook time:** 20 minutes **Serves:** 6-12 portions

150g caster sugar
150g butter
130g self-raising flour
20g cornflour
3 medium eggs
30ml milk
1 tsp vanilla extract
6 different food colours
sprinkles/decorations

Icing:
500g icing sugar
250g unsalted butter
1 tsp vanilla extract
3 tbsp milk

1. Preheat the oven to 160°C/Gas 3 and place 12 muffin/cupcake cases in a muffin tin.

2. Beat the sugar and butter with the vanilla essence until light and fluffy.

3. Add 1 egg, 1/3 of the flour and a splash of milk and beat until just combined. Then repeat until all the ingredients are used up.

4. Add 2 large spoons of the cake mixture to six zip-lock food bags, then add some food colouring to each one. Add a small amount at a time – it's very strong! Massage the mixture and the food colouring until you have the desired colour, adding more colour if required.

5. Starting with red (or any bright colour) snip the corner off the bag and squeeze a layer, covering the bottom of the cases. Then repeat with the other colours. Use a tooth pick to move the batter around (or the end of a tsp so as to cover the previous colour).

6. When you have completed all the colours bake in the oven for 25-30 minutes.

7. Remove and cool in the tins for 10 minutes before cooling on a wire rack.

For the icing:

1. Put all the ingredients into a large bowl and beat until smooth and shiny.

2. Once the rainbow cakes are cooked, spread or pipe onto the tops of the cupcakes.

3. To finish, decorate with sprinkles or decoration of your choice.

141

Jimmy & Jamian Lewis

Beetroot Lemon Seeded Cake

 Prep time: 20 minutes   **Cook time:** 55 minutes   **Serves:** 8 people

butter for greasing tin

350g self-raising flour

1 level tsp baking powder

½ tsp ground cinnamon

275ml sunflower oil

350g light muscavado sugar

3 eggs, separated

200g raw beetroot, peeled

juice of ½ a lemon

125g mix fruits (sultanas and raisins)

125g mixed seeds (sunflower, pumpkin)

icing (tub of ready made icing)

lemon jelly slices for decorating

1. Preheat the oven to 180°C/ Gas 4. Lightly grease and line a deep 8 inch cake tin.

2. Sift the flour, baking powder and cinnamon together, put aside. Beat the oil and sugar in a food processor, or by hand. Add the egg yolks one by one, mixing after adding each one.

3. Grate the beetroot and add it to the mixture, then add the lemon juice, mixed fruits and seeds, and pulse in a food processor, or mix by hand, until it is smooth.

4. Turn your food processor to low and add the flour mixture, or gently stir it in.

5. In another bowl, whisk the egg whites until nearly stiff. Using a metal spoon, fold the egg whites into the cake mixture (a wooden one will take the air out).

6. Put the mixture into the cake tin and bake for 25 minutes, cover the cake with foil and cook for another 30 minutes. Test it with a skewer to check if it is cooked – the skewer should come out clean.

7. Let the cake cool down for about 20 minutes.

8. Cut the cake in half and put icing in the middle of the cake and drizzle on top. Decorate with lemon jelly slices and maybe some raspberries.

Mackenzy, Franky & Jay Ruehle
CHOCOLATE BISCUIT COOKIES

 Prep time: 20 minutes   **Cook time:** 7-10 minutes   **Serves:** 8 people

65ml vegetable oil

25ml water

1 egg

200g choc chips

125g butter unsalted

1 ½ tsp vanilla essence

225g self-raising flour

½ tsp salt

100g sugar

16 creme filled chocolate cookies – we love Oreos!

1. Preheat the oven to 150°C/Gas 2. Place the butter and sugar in a large bowl. Add the egg and vanilla essence and mix well.

2. Sieve in the flour and salt and mix to combine well.

3. Add the chocolate chips and water and mix for 3 minutes.

4. Roll the mixture into balls. Squash the balls down gently, placing a chocolate biscuit on top, in the middle of the flattened ball. Then fold the mixture around the biscuit.

5. Spread the balls, with biscuits in the middle, evenly on a sheet of greaseproof paper.

6. Cook for 7-10 minutes until golden brown. Maybe drizzle a little melted chocolate over the top. Then break open and enjoy!

Georgia & Hannah Miles

DOUBLE CHOCOLATE BROWNIES

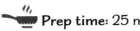 **Prep time:** 25 minutes   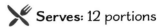 **Cook time:** 35 minutes   **Serves:** 12 portions

1 tsp vanilla extract

175g 70% good quality dark chocolate

50g good quality milk chocolate

225g unsalted butter, diced

3 free range eggs (medium)

225g caster sugar

30ml strong black coffee

75g self-raising flour

pinch of salt

100g of 70% chocolate broken into small pieces.

1. Preheat the oven to 140°C/ Gas 1.

2. Grease and line a 7 x 11in or 18 x 28cm baking tray.

3. Break the 175g 70% chocolate and the 50g milk chocolate into a microwave bowl.

4. Add the diced butter.

5. Melt in a microwave at 30 second intervals, stirring well in between, taking care not to burn the mixture (alternatively melt the mixture in a heatproof bowl over hot water).

6. Leave the mixture to cool for 5 minutes.

7. In a large bowl, beat the eggs, sugar, coffee and vanilla extract until smooth.

8. Slowly add the chocolate mixture to the eggs, sugar, coffee and vanilla extract until smooth.

9. Sift the flour and salt into the mixture.

10. Add the extra 100g 70% chocolate pieces.

11. Mix together, folding gently.

12. Spoon the mixture into the prepared tray and bake for 35 minutes.

13. Dust with icing sugar, if you like, or add a sprig of mint.

14. Serve warm or cool, chopped into squares or small pieces.

Georgia & Hannah Miles
S'MORES CHEESECAKE

 Prep time: 40 minutes   **Cook time:** 25 minutes   **Serves:** 12 portions

100g digestive biscuits

50g pretzels

70g butter, melted

250g cream cheese

250g ricotta

2 small eggs

1 tsp vanilla bean paste

200g condensed milk

200g chocolate chips (milk, white, dark – mixture of your choice)

white marshmallows or marshmallow fluff

Chocolate sauce

100g plain chocolate

30g butter

2 tbsp double cream plus extra for whipping

2 tbsp golden syrup

1. These little cheesecakes with digestive pretzel base and toasted marshmallow topping are just too tempting to resist – they are my favourite cheesecake recipe! For an extra special treat you can serve them with ice cream and hot chocolate sauce if you wish!

2. Crush the digestive biscuits and pretzels to very fine crumbs in a food processor or bash in a clean plastic bag with a rolling pin. Stir in the melted butter and mix well. Place a spoonful of the crumbs in each hole of a cheesecake pan, or 12 cupcake tin. Press down firmly using the end of a rolling pin, or the back of a small spoon, to smooth out the mixture.

3. Preheat the oven to 170°C/ Gas 3. Whisk together the cream cheese and ricotta. Add the eggs, vanilla and condensed milk and whisk again until smooth. Stir in three quarters of the chocolate chips. Pour the mixture into the 12 holes of the pan so that they are almost full. Depending on the size of your pan you may not need all of the mixture.

4. Bake for 20 to 25 minutes until set with a slight wobble. Remove the tin from the oven and sprinkle the remaining chocolate chips over the cheesecakes straight away so that they melt slightly whilst the cheesecakes are still warm.

5. Once cool, remove from the tin and chill in the refrigerator for several hours before serving.

6. To make the chocolate sauce, heat the chocolate, butter, cream and syrup in a saucepan until the chocolate has melted and the sauce is smooth and glossy.

7. Top the cheesecakes with the marshmallows and toast them lightly with a blowtorch or under the grill. Serve with the chocolate sauce and whipped cream or ice cream.

Thuan & Kelly Snowdon

HONEYCOMB CHEESECAKE

 **Prep time:** 30 minutes **Cook time:** 4 hours ✗ **Serves:** 8 people

For the base:

300g crushed digestive biscuits

115g unsalted butter, melted and slightly cooled

For the cheesecake:

400g full fat cream cheese

180ml double cream

70g caramel sauce

120g icing sugar, sifted

1 tsp vanilla extract

150g chocolate honeycomb pieces

85g milk chocolate, melted

For the honeycomb:

100g caster sugar

3 tbsp golden syrup

1 tsp bicarbonate of soda

1. Grease and line a 9 inch round, spring form cake tin. Place biscuit crumbs into a medium sized bowl and pour the melted butter over the crumbs.

2. Mix until all the crumbs are covered in butter, then tip into your greased pan and press into the pan until you have a level biscuit layer. Place in the fridge, whilst you make the cheesecake.

3. Place the cream cheese, double cream, caramel sauce, icing sugar and vanilla extract into a large bowl and beat until light and smooth.

4. Add in the chocolate covered honeycomb pieces and fold in by hand.

5. Take your chilled base out of the fridge and then pour your cheesecake filling over the top. Smooth until level.

6. Place in the fridge for around 4 hours, until firm.

7. Whilst the cheesecake is chilling, make the honeycomb: line a baking tray with grease-proof paper and leave to one side.

8. Place the sugar and golden syrup into a medium sized saucepan, over a low heat. Stir occasionally until the sugar dissolves and the mixture starts to get runny. Then stop stirring.

9. Once the mixture starts bubbling around the edges, turn the heat up to high and boil until golden – this will take about 5 minutes. Lift the pan and give it a swirl every so often to stop it burning, but do not stir.

10. Once the entire mixture is golden yellow (don't let it get dark and caramel coloured, this is overdone), remove from heat and add in bicarbonate of soda immediately. The mixture will froth up very quickly and then settle. Once the bicarb has dissolved, the mixture will stop expanding. Pour it onto your lined baking tray and leave to set completely.

11. Once set, break into shards and leave to one side whilst you finish off the cheesecake.

12. Remove the cheesecake from the fridge and place the melted chocolate into a squeezy bottle or small sandwich bag, with the corner snipped off.

13. Drizzle the chocolate all over the top of your cheesecake, however you like.

14. Take small shards of honeycomb and place around the edge of your cheesecake and in the centre, however many pieces you want.

15. Place back into the fridge until ready to serve. Serve with fresh strawberries.

Kai & Chris Lee

Oat Bran Muffins

 **Prep time:** 15 minutes   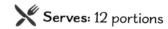 **Cook time:** 17 minutes   **Serves:** 12 portions

1 small packet oat bran

100g wholemeal self-raising flour

1 rounded dessert spoon baking powder

50g brown sugar

½ packet dates

50g chopped walnuts

50g sultanas (optional)

2 egg whites

500ml skimmed or semi-skimmed milk

2 tbsp olive oil

1 tsp vanilla essence

Optional

2 tsp ground ginger

3 tsp cocoa

1. Preheat the oven to 220°C/Gas 7. Mix together the oat bran, wholemeal flour, baking powder and brown sugar.

2. Chop the dates and the walnuts into small pieces and add to the dry mixture. Mix in the sultanas if you want extra fruity muffins (for Ginger Muffins add 2 tsp ground ginger, or for Chocolate Muffins add 3 tsp cocoa).

3. Into a separate jug pour the milk, olive oil, egg whites and vanilla essence.

4. Pour the liquid into the dry mixture and stir well.

5. Pour into 12 (or more) bun tins and place into the oven for 17 minutes or less depending on depth of bun tins.

6. Store in a plastic bag and keep refrigerated.

7. These can be eaten warm by putting them in the microwave for 15 seconds – delicious!

8. By not using the yolk of egg, you've saved yourself 340mg of cholesterol!

THE PEOPLE AND CHEFS WHO MADE COOKS & KIDS POSSIBLE

We have had so much help and fun with *Cooks & Kids 3*, but none of it would have been possible without the help of all our supporters who have given their time and their talent freely and without cost to help ensure we raise as much money as possible for Place2Be.

THE CHILDREN

There were lots of children and young people who wanted to help with Cooks & Kids and we have been unable to feature all of them and their recipes in this edition but we can say a huge thank you to them all that joined in the fun at our 'cook offs' - they were fantastic! They chopped and stirred, they got messy, they got the chefs messy and they learned a lot - you were all, quite frankly, amazing:

Amber, Austin, Ben, Bethan, Bethany, Declan, Elliot, Emma, Franky, Georgia, Isobel, Jacob, Jamie, Jimmy, Kai, Katrina, Kelsie, Leala, Leo, Lucy, Macie, Mackenzy, Madison, Marie, Naht, Neil, Nia, Sanna, Sarah, Shannon, Steven, Thuan and Zahra.

THE NFA GROUP STAFF

Managing a time and talent project like Cooks & Kids takes a lot of time and commitment, and yet again the NFA Group staff and the Corporate Social Responsibility team worked tirelessly to make it all happen:

Liz Cowling, Louise Bouckley, Zazie Chesters, Iain Owens, Kate Davis, Krishane Madhaven, Tamzin Roberts, Kerri Harris, Rhiannon Flindall, Tamzin Salisbury and Katherine Lyall.

We would also like to give a special mention to the NFA Group Marketing team who have all worked relentlessly on this project and, without their consistent hard work, Cooks & Kids wouldn't have been possible. Thank you to Andrew Isaac, Julie-Anne Jordan, Robert Shaw, Fiona Barnes and Sue Barlow.

THE PHOTOGRAPHERS

We cannot thank these people enough for their patience and their willingness to use their great artistic talent to take some truly awesome shots of Cooks & Kids in production. Led by the amazing Miranda Parry from Miranda Parry Photography (www.mirandaparry.com), their artistic talent and professional skills can be seen throughout the book and on the Cooks & Kids website. A huge thank you to Miranda Parry, Sam Peat and Clare McGregor.

We would also like to give an extra mention to Matthew Gyton, currently studying A Level photography, who came along and took some great shots and even got the chance to cook with one of the celebrity chefs!

Lastly, thank you to our videographer, Duncan Smith, who filmed all of the cooking sessions and edited the videos into fantastic short films which have been uploaded to the Cooks & Kids website, YouTube and social media channels.

THE VENUE

AVEQIA provided Cooks & Kids with a brilliant venue in which all of the Cooks & Kids photoshoots and cooking sessions took place. When we initially approached Aveqia, they jumped at the chance to contribute to a programme which encourages kids to take part in improving their skills in the kitchen, whilst understanding about different ingredients and learning from the celebrity chefs.

We would like to thank both Paul Vines and Sam Imlay from AVEQIA who provided us with fundamental support throughout.

GRAFFEG

Graffeg provided the book design, editorial and production expertise. Thanks to Lauren Sourbutts for copy editing and Joana Rodrigues for design and especially Peter Gill for his support throughout this great project.

EVERYONE ELSE!

It was wonderful to see so many people willing and wanting to get involved with this project, so a special mention goes out to Libby Wallace, Robert Jordan, Harry Smith, Isobel Smith, Sandy Lacey-Aberdein and Edie Chesters who all gave their time for free to provide support.

GREGG WALLACE

TV presenter known for *MasterChef, Celebrity MasterChef, MasterChef: The Professionals.* He regularly writes for *Good Food* and *Olive* magazine and is the author of several books. Gregg is passionate about supporting Cooks & Kids and has used his talents to bring so many smiles to so many people.

MICHEL ROUX JR

Two-star Michelin Chef at London restaurant La Gavroche. He is the son of Albert Roux, one of the Roux Brothers who opened La Gavroche in 1967. He has appeared on *Gordon Ramsey's Hell's Kitchen,* as an expert judge on *MasterChef: The Professionals* and BBC2's *Food and Drink.*

ALDO ZILLI

Award-winning chef and restaurateur, specialising in Italian cuisine. Has appeared on several TV series including *Celebrity Fit Club, Big Brother's Little Brother, Lorraine Kelly's Big Fat Challenge.*

CHRIS LEE

Kent-born Chris Lee and his wife Hayley run the award-winning The Bildeston Crown. Chris attained a 3 AA Rosette status and was named an 'up-and-coming' chef in the *Good Food Guide*. The Bildeston Crown has also won Suffolk Restaurant of the Year.

CYRUS TODIWALA

OBE DL DBA

Celebrity television chef who previously cooked for Queen Elizabeth II and Prince Philip, Duke of Edinburgh as part of the Diamond Jubilee celebrations. Has appeared on *Saturday Kitchen, Daybreak* and regular slots on BBC Radio 4, Radio 5 Live and BBC World Service. Owner of several restaurants in London.

GILL MOSS

Gill is the sous chef at De Vere Whites hotel where she has worked for 11 years. She always wanted to become a chef and had a great time cooking with the kids for this book. The dishes she cooked were simple and healthy but also interesting for children to make.

ERIC ALLOUARD

Head Chef at AVEQIA London. A French chef who has worked in a string of Michelin and top class restaurants around the world.

HANNAH MILES

MasterChef finalist 2007, Hannah now writes cookery columns for two magazines and has published more than 13 cookbooks.

JAMIAN LEWIS

Executive Head Chef at CCT Venues. Jamian says 'This was a fantastic opportunity for me to work with the kids. As a parent myself I love to educate and inspire through food. It is also a great way to teach children about the importance of a balanced diet.'

JOHN WOODWARD

John is the Executive Head Chef for De Vere Venues, and helped all of our budding chefs during the Cooks & Kids cookery days. Fanatical about food, John has had a diverse career; starting under acclaimed chefs such as the Roux brothers before travelling and working in Australia and operating in the venue sector.

KELLY SNOWDON

Kelly has been working with De Vere Venues for 6 years. She has been Head Chef for 3 years and currently works at West One in London.

MICHIEL BOEREBOOM

Michiel is Head Chef at Devonport House. Ever since he was 13 he has been working in professional kitchens throughout Europe.

JAY RUEHLE

Jay previously worked as a chef in Los Angeles with Wolfgang Puck and is now the head chef at The Royal Clifton Hotel and Spa in Southport.

JOLYON YATES

Jolyon has been Head Chef at Warbrook House for 4 years. He says 'A career of a chef is not just a job but a life style choice.'

PETER BAYLESS

Winner of *MasterChef* 2006. He published *My Father Could Only Boil Cornflakes* before going on to work at La Gavroche. He now cooks at a variety of UK & French restaurants, writes for food magazines and teaches at cookery schools.

ROGER RAHAMAN

Roger swapped a successful career in media sales and marketing to follow his passion for food and cooking in the late 90's. He trained at the critically acclaimed gastro pub The Havelock Tavern and progressed to running the kitchen as Head Chef. Under his charge in 2009 the establishment was awarded a Michelin Bib Gourmand.

SIMON WOOD

Winner of *MasterChef* 2015. Author of *At Home with Simon Wood* and Executive Chef at Oldham Athletic.

PING COOMBES

Winner of *MasterChef* 2014. She has just been appointed Consultant Chef of Chi Kitchen, the pan-Asian restaurant in Debenhams' flagship Oxford Street store in London.

SARA DANESIN MEDIO

An Italian-born chef and *MasterChef* 2011 finalist and now a well known chef and food consultant.

SOPHIE THOMPSON

An actress and winner of *Celebrity MasterChef* 2014. TV and film appearances include *Four Weddings and a Funeral,* *Harry Potter, Eat Pray Love, Casualty, Eastenders* along with many theatre roles.

TOM DELL

Tom has worked for De Vere Venues for 15 years starting as an apprentice chef on an NVQ basis and working his way through the business to achieve his goal of becoming Head Chef. He has been Head Chef at Highfield Park for the last 5 years. Recently sold, Highfield Park is now an independent hotel embarking on a new and exciting adventure.

TOM KERRIDGE

Tom Kerridge and his wife Beth opened The Hand and Flowers in 2005 and it is now the only UK pub to be awarded two Michelin stars. Tom is now a celebrity chef who has appeared on the *Great British Menu*, *MasterChef*, *Saturday Kitchen* and currently presents *Food and Drink* and *Bake Off: Crème de la Crème* on BBC Two.

WAYNE SLEEP OBE

Wayne Sleep is a British dancer, director, choreographer, actor and panellist. He was previously a Principal Dancer with the Royal Ballet. He appeared on the 2014 series of *Celebrity MasterChef* alongside Sophie Thompson, narrowly missing out on a place in the final.

MORE ABOUT THE COOKS & KIDS BOOK SERIES

When we first talked to Alan Rustad ARC and Andrew Isaac NFA Group about a cookbook for kids, they were hooked on the idea right from the start.

The first book was a great success for everyone; the kids, the cooks, the readers, and of course the charity 'Magic Breakfast', who received the royalties. This third book written by kids for kids is just as exciting and full of fresh ideas for recipes as the first book. We hope you enjoy these recipes as much as we have enjoyed putting the book together for you.

Cooks & Kids: 11 top chefs and children cook up a storm in the kitchen with their favourite recipes

If you'd like a copy of either Cooks & Kids, Cooks & Kids Too or Cooks & Kids 3 in digital format – ebooks or apps – these will be available soon on our website **www.graffeg.com**

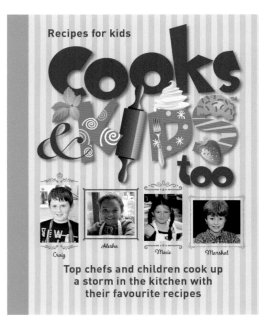

Recipes for kids

Top chefs and children cook up a storm in the kitchen with their favourite recipes

WWW.NFA.CO.UK
WWW.COOKSANDKIDS.COM